Healing The Spirit Inside Out

by Mary Wright

Healing The Spirit Inside Out

Shadow Production Publishing
28 Industrial street
Unit 120
East York
Ontario, Canada
M4G 1Y9

Canadian Cataloguing in Publication Data.

Main entry under title: Healing The Spirit Inside Out
First edition

ISBN 0-9683359-6-9

Dedication

I dedicate this book to the Spirit of the universe, and to the future generations that will begin to love each other in spite of colour, culture and country of origin.

At the time of printing of this book, someone or someones decided to destroy The World Trade Center and the Pentagon, killing thousands of people in the process. I cannot imagine the hearts of the people filled with such cancer of hatred that they would want to kill themselves and in the process use commercial airlines to perpetrate their crime.

The world now knows more so than ever that the spirit of man needs healing. Cancer is not a physical thing, it is in the spirit of the heart which is in need of healing. By asking the Divine to soften our hearts so that the soul can connect to the spirit to make us one, we can then become integrated and whole.

This week, I have been reading *Love and Awaking* by John Welwood. He said, "Spiritual work brings freedom, but soulful work brings integration." Both are necessary for a complete human life. When I listen to people talking about the bombing and who did it, I wonder why the spirits of men are talking like that before we know who really did it. I am shocked to see how deep the cancer of the spirit runs in peoples' hearts. One more shocking thing is listening to people who claim to be Christian and hearing them calling in on the radio talk shows. What they were saying frightens me. I am praying that this cancer of the spirit will be healed by all of us who are left behind to take a deeper look inside out.

Acknowledgments

Many thanks to the people who have been listening to me rambling on and on about this book, even before I put words on paper. Without the Spirit of the father, I know that I could not write this book -- there were so many challenges once I started writing it.

I wish to express a great, big thank you to all those mentioned below. First, to Hazel O'Loughlin-Vidal for her full-time editing and all her input on creativity, her prayers and layout skills. Thank you to the poetry group at the Atkinson Faculty of Liberal and Professional Studies for letting me read my poems. Without the group, I would not have met Hazel. Thanks again to Kay Finer for her support and her guidance in helping sort the book and arranging the contents so that it flowed. And to Ron Finer for allowing me to drop in his home and invade it, and no matter how tired he was, drive me home from Oshawa to Toronto late at night, Thank you! To Maureen Smith, my music teacher who taught me how to really look at the personalities, how they work and how many parts there are to a human being. Also, thanks to Justin Blayney for creating the cover, to Trey Johnson and Jason Embank for the photographs, and to Mothersill Printing. And of course, "The Shadow" who always directed me as to what to write, and which relevant books to read.

Table of Contents

Introduction

Dear Cancer,

Good Evening!

I have wanted to write you a letter for a long time, but I didn't have the courage to do so. I was so afraid of you that I kept putting off writing to you.

Finally, with my heart beating faster and faster, I found the courage to write to you, because I am no longer afraid of you! I have watched you for the last thirty years wreaking havoc in the lives of people. Gradually and systematically, you gained power and control over the world.

You have taken the world by storm, spreading your venom like wild fire over the minds and bodies. I don't know where you came from – what I do know is that you don't care about class, colour, or creed. You attack all with a vengeance – even our pets succumb to you.

You came in such a subtle way in people's lives. You caught them off-guard when they were not paying attention. You know we are so disconnected from our hearts, mind and spirit. We are too busy making money, and looking outside of ourselves for answers. When you moved in on us, we were not aware until you were all over us. You captured our bodies from the top of our head to the soles of our feet. What is so troubling to me, however, is the places you chose to initiate your attack.

First, it was the cervix, then it was the uterus. Those inner body parts have killed our women for the last fifty years. The last twenty years you have attacked the breasts, lungs, and colon. And now you are all over the bodies of women, but not only women, now your thrills are men's sexual organs, the prostate and the testes, and now the colon. What I don't understand however is, "why children and babies?"

You are in total control of everyone's lives. You also have aliases so that no one can even trace you. Why do you have such control? Is it the twenty billion dollars per year that makes you the center of attention in research, or the other twenty billion in pharmaceutical medicine?

You like it when people carry you around in their bodies because you raise billions and billions of dollar for doctors and scientists. Oh, I believe you are all about money -- that is why there is yet no cure.

When I was a little girl, I moved to a small village in St. Thomas, east of Kingston, Jamaica in the West Indies. People in our little village used to complain about boils under their arms, between their grains, or in any soft places, but mostly on the neck and underarms. I did not know that you are the lesion that North Americans called "Cancer." I thought those boils were just cyclical lesions. My mother and father used to get them often, and my father used to really take care of himself. He used to purge his blood regularly, because he said that if they got inside the body, the blood would get infected and he would die. My father said, "blood is the life force of a man, and if the blood is infected, it's hard to get rid of the infection." Every morning, we would first have a cup of herbal tea (or bush tea as it was called) before anything else got into the stomach. With the herbal tea, in no time the boils would be gone.

I didn't know that you could turn inside and cause people to be sick unto death. *Why are you here?* Cancer, are you here to teach us a lesson, on how to pay attention to our spirit, and to commit our life to the source? Cancer, are you capitalizing on the fact that we have lost consciousness of what our purpose in this life is all about? Cancer, we have been so stressed out for the last fifty years, and it has gotten worse every year since. We have built big corporations, governments, big houses and great businesses, and we even sent men and women in space. The more we have, the more we build without stopping to connect to the spirit of the heart and soul. We are so afraid of ourselves that we are afraid to go to sleep at night. Most of us are so pilled out for stress or for sleep. Yet, for all the research that has been done, we haven't been able to find a cure for you. Is it because there's too much money to be made from you being here or perhaps pharmaceutical companies don't want you to go away because you generate so much money throughout the world?

Cancer, the world organization is having trouble with you. You are out of control, and the establishment of the world does not know how to get rid of you. You just seem like you are here to stay, especially since you now have company. You have AIDS, Parkinson, heart dis-ease, TB, multiple-sclerosis, and diabetes, and the list goes on and on. Cancer, we are going to take back control of our lives. Tell us when you are leaving, and I will be the first to announce to the world that you are gone — instead of hearing on the tv commercials that sixty thousand Canadian women will be diagnosed with breast cancer, and five thousand will die this year. We are so brain washed to think the worst of ourselves — we are out of touch with our feelings, our bodies, mind, soul, and heart. Cancer, when you leave the world, we will celebrate from our souls with the joy and peace you have stolen from us. The fear of you will be lifted from the souls of men, women, boys, girls, teenagers and most of all babies who will grow up to be productive human beings.

Thank you, Cancer. It is good to write to you.

Goodbye, In love,

Mary Wright

Dear People of the world:

I got your letters, but I notice that even though I took so many lives, you are still behaving and mistreating your bodies the same way you always have — rushing and running after more things, still stressed out and not eating and taking care of yourselves. From generation to generation, you have not taken care of yourselves.

Your spirits are yours alone, not to hand over to your doctors. You still believe in the scientists to find a cure for you. You put all your trust in the doctors who are human beings like yourselves. The only way I will leave you alone is when you stop focusing on the external rather than the internal, the heart and soul. People, you are still stressed out — you don't treat each other with respect. Your heart is full of hate. Your food is eaten in a hurry, and you are not going anywhere — always on the run. You don't take time out to say thanks to the Creator, and when you do, it is to ask for more things.

People, you want your heart, soul and spirit to be healed, but you are not willing to trust the Father who created you, but you are willing to put your trust in man and governments who can neither heal, nor help you.

People of the world, I want you to know that I was created in a lab in the name of research — by man. Those little tumors as new names were fed with different chemicals -- that's why I became a killer. The only way a cure will come is when you connect your minds, emotions, and souls to the Spirit of the creator, which is the father. Then and only then, you will see a cure for all dis-eases. Thank you for writing to me.

Your new friend,

Cancer

Chapter 1

Healing

Cancer is in our face every time I turn on the tv. And they just keep it revived in our consciousness so that we do not lose the fear of being sick. I do not know who in my family had cancer, but now I heard that my son might have cancer in his lungs. I do not know if it is because I wanted to write about healing. Healing is more than just finding a cure for illness. Finding cures for any dis-ease is not healing. Healing is from the soul and the Spirit of the universe. That is what real healing is all about. Finding cures for dis-eases is a business where a lot of money can be made. Cancer is a money-making dis-ease. It brings in millions of dollars per year. Why would pharmaceutical companies want to keep people sick — so that they can make money off them. Cancer, like all illnesses is not of the body, but of the spirit. It just manifests itself through the body because there is no other outlet for dis-ease to show itself.

Healing the Inside

True healing can only take place from the inside. Healing the spirit is not the same as the healing that takes place in the mind. There are many levels where healing has to take place in order for someone to say I am cured of Cancer, or TB or of any one of the other dis-eases. Once I saw a man talking to my son, and he wanted him to go with him upstairs in the attic in the old house where we were living on Palmerston ave. I was shocked, I told my son that he could fall off the roof.

I was sitting at my sewing machine and he was getting ready for work. He was seventeen years old. I would never want my enemy to experience what I had been through that day. The level and intensity of emotions were unbearable. It was a new high of whatever it was happening to me. I cannot imagine what was going on in his mind. I just sat hanging my head down on the machine and I prayed. "Dear Father, help Geoffrey to know which spirit is talking to him." I said that prayer over and over until he went off to work. Was Geoffrey afraid of going to jail? I would never know. All I know is that from that day forward, he was never the same again.

I used to watch the television healing service by Oral Roberts. I would sit for hours watching Oral Roberts and all the other religious programs on laying on of hands on people to be healed. I love Oral Roberts. I believed in what he was talking about because my mother had TB and I prayed for her healing, and she was healed to the point where she was sent home after five years of being hospitalized.

In 1972, I went to Jamaica for a visit. I went to the church that I used to attend when I lived there. I met a friend of mine that I used to associate with. I knew how to pray, and I used to pray for all kinds of people and miracles used to occur. Back then, I was involved with God. I was invited to go and have lunch with her daughter-in-law. Since her son got married and immigrated to the United States, the daughter-in-law had not been able to walk. The church had been praying. I had been praying — nothing happened. After lunch, we went into the living room to talk and pray. I laid hands on the daughter-in-law. I called on the great healer whom I knew since childhood. I was taught how to call on God for help. Today, I do not call the Spirit, God. Because of growing intimacy, I call the Spirit of the universe, Father. I then returned to Canada, not thinking anything about the healing of her daughter-in-law. Later, her mother-in-law wrote me to encourage me to keep on with the ministry of healing, because her daughter got healed and went to the United States. I have never practised the laying on of hands again. I just pray for people. I first pray for myself and ask for help from the Spirit of the father. I was taught how to pray and ask for help when I could barely speak. My parents belonged to no church, but I had a nanny who was very spiritual.

People used to be spiritual before there was any Christianity. Today, everyone is a Christian or religious person. When I talk about spirituality to Christian people, the attitude is one of, "You're going to hell." Or when I say the Spirit of the creator, I am looked upon like a witch. We are so programmed to think the way the church fathers wanted us to think, it is incredible.

Take Jesus for instance, the church fathers have been preaching for centuries that Jesus died for our sins. But when I was watching Oral Roberts, I believed that too. However, when my eyes opened to my soul, and my heart was in a place of learning, I was still in need of healing. I know that Jesus did not die for my sin. Jesus was hanged for showing the people the truth, and the people that were in power were terrified of the truth, because back then the religious leaders of the day did not want to change the way things were done. It is much like today, all the various church leaders do not want to change to the way Jesus presented, so they formed big organizations in which everyone has to follow the rules and abide by the rules. The rules are like this, preach to the people and tell them that Jesus died for their sin, absolving them of all responsibility for their lives. That was what Jesus was trying to put across to the people, and that was what he was hanged for.

Last fall season, when I started to write the piece on healing, I did not know that I was writing about my son, and that he was in need of spiritual healing. He came to visit me for Thanksgiving. We talked for three days about what he wanted to do with his life, or I should say I did most of the talking and he listened. One year later, I am the one doing the visiting. I went with him to talk to his doctor to hear if he had lung cancer. Life has a way of telling us what to do and say at the right time, but if we are too busy looking outside of ourselves to hear what our spirit is saying to us, why should the outside forces not make the decision for us? If we are too tired to listen to what our hearts and bodies are saying to us, anything will overtake us. My son is so afraid of life, and so he chose to be sick. I believe that he created his own dis-ease by allowing the external power to take over the energy of the soul because of his fear. He is so angry at life, because his dad rejected him and I raised him on my own. He was also a very self-centered person, to the point where, by the time he was seventeen years old, he had five nervous breakdowns.

Looking back at my son since he was a little boy, he was always sick with pneumonia, which led up to a nervous breakdown. He was born with a sick spirit, or a splinter personality. I have just learned about splintered personalities. I had learned a long time ago about the fragmented soul. At the time when I was reading about souls, I did not know that there was such a thing as a fragmented soul, but it is not the soul, it is the different part of us as human beings, or what we call personalities. I do not think that the soul can be sick, but I guess that when the energy of the soul which is the power of the soul is gone, the spirit will leave because it becomes disconnected from the source which is the universe. My son is disconnected from the source which is the universe. That is how the external powers of the society are able to control others.

My son could not handle what the external powers wanted of him, so he made himself sick, that he would not be responsible for himself or his actions. Fear kept him for most of his young life angry at me, his dad, and I believe, at the whole world. And now at thirty-one, he is now facing cancer that can send his soul home prematurely without his soul learning what it came to earth to learn. My son is so creative and bright, but he does not know how to bring that creativity from the inside, to pull out that creative spirit and let it direct him to keep on the road of life, and to pick himself up when life knocks him down. Life did knock him down when he was young. He started to run with boys that did not like the external law, and so he got into a lot of conflict with the police. Growing up in Canada is not easy for any one, especially being a black man. The so-called external power decided that if people have a different colour, they are not human beings. If a black man ever showed any sign of wanting something different, the powers would be all over him.

The last run-in with the police was the last straw. What Geoffrey did not know was that his soul came to earth to learn its lesson. No matter what, you cannot give away the spirit or the energy of the soul. All kinds of dis-ease will manifest itself in the body, because it Is the only place where one can feel sick. The pain of the spirit is very hard on the soul, especially when it is not connected to the universe. That is why every time I turn around, cancer is in our face, and I keep asking the same question over and over, "Why are there so many cancer victims when there is so much awareness about the dis-ease today, in the newspapers, on the radio, television, and the Internet. The more we talk about it, it seems like the more it spreads. It is on everyone's lips. I believe that the reason why we talk about cancer so much is that it will derive more money for the Canadians and the worldwide cancer society. It is not just cancer, but there is heart disease, diabetes, AIDS, TB and the list goes on.

Surrender

I have a big challenge with surrendering my life to the creator, because I had been given the authority to take control of my parents', my sisters', and brothers' lives when my papa left my mama with five small children in Winchester District of St. Thomas, Jamaica. It was shortly after WWII, when people were just trying to put back their lives together. Then, in the midst of all this, there came a hurricane in 1951. I was seven years old. Papa left and someone had to fill his place. I did. I became the man of the house and brought some level of normalcy to our house.

Surrendering my will to the unknown was one of the hardest things I have ever done, but as time goes by, I realize that if I did not let go and let the creator help me, I would not be here today. I also raised four children on my own, so yes, I am very controlling. I had to decide who was going to run my home and tell my four children what they could or/and could not do. When you get that kind of control at such an early age, yes, controlling others is a given. There is no one on earth that was as controlling as I was, but I do not want dis-eases of all kinds, and I know that I could lose the energy of the soul by spending so much time telling others what to do when my life and home need to be straightened out.

So many people that are in power today are experiencing much disarray in their lives, yet they are running the society and ruling people. No wonder the people of the world are so lost inside, because the people who are governing them are from a society of dis-eases of the heart and mind. Their emotional and their mental lives are so immature that the people they govern are lost.

Serenity comes when one's life is surrendered to the creator through the emotional and mental maturity, and that only happens by giving over control to the love and power of the universal Spirit of the whole earth. Serenity also brings joy, peace and harmony to the soul so that it can learn its lesson of this life. Serenity or surrender is how we as people who say they love the energy of the spirit, honour the creator of the universe. Honouring through serenity by surrender is how I learned to let go of failed relationships. After not trusting the creator

5

wholeheartedly, and a series of great losses, I was so tired of crying and complaining that I just handed all the pain of controlling to Father.

I also learned that prayer is the key to surrendering to Father. So, one day I started to pray. "Father," I said, "please take this load off my shoulder. I don't want to control other people's lives any more. You can do a better job than I can. Father, I am a big failure. I don't want to tell people what to do, but I pray that you will speak to their spirit so that things will change for them."

Letting go of that power was not easy for me — it is still a struggle at times, but today I know now how to ask the father for his or her wisdom to help others. Thanks to surrendering that spirit of that loving energy we call love.

Healing the soul through that love also brings healing to cancer, AIDS, TB and all those other dis-eases that we face to day. Without surrendering, love cannot go through the body. Healing comes from the centre of our being, and when there is no connection through centering of the energy, how can we be whole? True healing comes from our being in the middle of the universal whole.

Chapter 2

The Creator

What is the Creator? And who is the Creator? And where did the universe and life begin? Where did it all begin? These are all the questions I began to ask myself. And why is it so important for me to ask these questions?

For centuries upon centuries, man like myself, has been asking all kind of questions. And for others who think they have the answer to other men's questions, I do not believe that anyone has the true answer to this question, when it come to the "Creator" or about life.

The Creator is a mystery to me and to everyone. I look at everything around me and I know that I did not create the things I see around me such as the moon, stars and all people, trees and even the tiniest creeping things around. When I look at the various kinds of flowers, plants and trees — at the many differences such as the fruits they bear, and the grass, I sometimes stop and talk to the invisible creator, of how beautiful the flowers, trees, grass and all creation is. When something happens to me that I was unprepared for, I give thanks to the creator of the universe.

The Creator, to me, is this invisible mysterious energy that no one can see with the naked eye or hear without quietness. This quietness comes from a place that only you or I can go to individually. It comes from the heart and mind. The heart alone cannot do it. It must be with the mind also, so that one is complete in him or herself to see from the inside. The in-visible is of the heart, and the mysterious is of the mind. When the heart, soul, and mind get together, there is a constant communication to give whatever we call life balance or harmony with the creator. The creator is life in its total balance of communication where respect, trust, and truth (which is love) give peace of mind with joy in the soul. It is also where the soul can learn the purpose for which it came to earth.

Creativity

Creativity — what about it? It is our imagination, or as my teacher who used to walked across the one-roomed school house over to me when I was a little girl portrayed. "Mary Wright," she would call loudly, and every child in that one-roomed school-house would scream out, "She is caught day dreaming again." They would ask me what I caught that day and then laugh. Children have a sense of who they are. They are very creative. Creativity is the source of the invisible to the visible. It is what the creator handed down to man to keep us connected to the divine.

Man is created in the image of the creator, and the likeness of the Divine, and therein lies the mystery of creation. We are therefore primarily creative beings. Our sexuality is secondary. We do not share our sexuality with the Creator, but with the created. We are then to honour the Divine in our daily lives by being extremely creative. Our intense sexual drives as human beings are not always to be satisfied, but to be transmuted into creativity. This is one of the essential differences between human and beast. Why then is sex so important in our lives? Why do we promote billion dollar businesses based on sexual behavior? Why then does society favour cognitive over creative living? Is not our right brain hemisphere equal in importance to our left brain hemisphere? Could it be a deliberate conspiracy to atrophy that which connects us with our creator? Could the excessive imagery of sexuality played out in the air waves be a tool to systematically reduce man's purpose? Sexuality is temporal, creativity is eternal.

Man from generation to generation has created some ugliness in their lives, such as jealousy, and jealousy creates fear, anger, dis-ease, hunger and ultimately, war. Our thoughts should unfold into words, into deeds, and actions create power, joy, peace, and love. Power has become negatively unfolded into control, and not the creativity that power was divinely created to be. Power was never created to control the universe, but a lack of understanding of what creativity is all about, is why the world has turned its attention to the sexual revolution.

Artistic creativity is only a minute part of creativity. All creation begins with thought, through the father of creation —

then the spoken word. When I read Iyanla Vanzant's, "One Day When My Soul Just Opened Up," and when I read the piece on creativity, I realized I should honor the Divine with Creativity. "What! Honor the Divine with Creativity?" was my reaction. I thought I had read everything there is to know, but I did not know anything about honoring the father. Religion talks about praising and worshiping the father(God). I have been on this path of wanting to know since I was five, and when I turned thirty, I took a hundred and eighty degree turn to my life. I started to read all kinds of different books other than the bible or books on Christianity or Judaism. The Bible was not enough any more. I wanted to satisfy my soul with relevant and applicable literature. I was so hungry for information about soul growing and learning. It was like I had never eaten for a year. That is how hungry I was inside.

I understand why people who say they are artistic drink, smoke, take drugs and use sex for artistic expression. There are mental, emotional and spiritual hungers, and nothing outside of you or me can fill that emptiness that comes upon us. When I bought Iyanla Vanzant's book, I thought I knew, and learned a lot about life, but this was new to me. I must remember to honor the Divine through right thinking each day. Only the Divine creates true healing. Creativity is healing the mental, emotional and most of all spiritual. The soul(spirit) is the image of the creator that divinely guides us through the creative process.

Chapter 3

Art

Art is a creative energy that should penetrate the soul. It can manifest itself in various forms, such as singing, writing, communicating, acting, painting and designing. Healing is a part of the art community, but only if it comes from the soul, or the spirit.

When I was a little girl, I loved to talk, and when I had an asthma attack, sometime I would find it very hard to talk, but I would always sing even if it was just a hum. I would hum until I could breathe again. Why are so many people in our society so sick today? People are living longer yet, they are so sick. I do not know why? I do not have the answer for the why's, but I do know that we as people, in our society, have left our creative energy some place, hoping that at a later date, we can come back and pick up from where we left off. The spirit of creativity is not something one can put aside and come back later to put it back together again so easily. Life is not like that, one either works with their creativity or one does not.

Singing, writing, sewing and speaking are where I put my soul. The energy of the soul has a need to express itself through us, so we can learn that the universe sends the soul to sing its praise. Everyone in this life inherits the same energy of love. That energy which makes the grass grow, and the moon to emerge each month, and without this energy, there is no creativity. Music is from the soul, and that is why people who are often sick, love to listen to music. Music is healing to the soul. The spirit needs the music to allow the body to respond to the source, so it can be made whole.

Black people love to dance and sing. White people make fun of us singing and dancing. Do you know that if it was not for the singing and dancing of the black people, perhaps they would not have survived the hardship and slavery of the past. That is how their souls were able to transcend their situations. The white man did not abuse the body per se, it was the energy of the soul by beating on the spirit. But the black people had learned that to be healed, one must praise the universe through the energy of the soul. Today, we as black people do not sing the way we used to sing. Maybe it is because everything we do in terms of the art, the white man took over and made it theirs. It is about money for the white man. For the blacks, creativity and art are for the sake of the soul — its healing of the pain and fear that sits in the soul. It was the reason why the black people sang.

I remember when I was a little girl, we always sang. If we were happy or sad, we would sing. My mother was always sick, but come evening, and the six of us children and my mother would sit and sing for two hours. My mother used to say no matter what is happening in our lives, we must praise the universe for its love, because without the spirit of the creator, no man would be on the earth. I took that to heart, that was the gospel according to what my mother said. I love to sing and I love music. When I am challenged and I want answers, I just sit quietly and hum a song, even when I do not feel like it.

The universe needs us to praise it, and we need the universe to heal us through our singing of praise to it. If there are so many dis-eases in the world, and so many people singing, why is there no healing coming forth? I believe it is because people are not really singing from the heart and soul, or for the right reason. When the reason is only money, then it is not for the right reason, and it is not coming from the soul. When it is from the soul, the joy is there, the energy is what does the healing.

Anything in this life that takes the fun and joy out of the arts, no matter what it is, then it is just mechanical. Most of what we do today is so mechanical that it has lost its taste. So, how can music and singing heal the soul when life is mechanical. The one thing in this life is not mechanical is the universe and the earth itself. Nature will never be mechanical, neither is man. Man thinks he is mechanical because that is how society want us to be. So when our bodies show any sign of sickness and dis-ease, right away man wants to cure the body without the Spirit. Without the Spirit, there are no bodies, and music and singing and dancing can resurrect the soul or the spirit and connect it back to the universe.

The Seasons

The world used to run by the four Seasons, winter, spring, summer, and fall. Man changed it by time: day, month and year. The universe still runs by season. Even though man would like things to be the way man wants it to be, it is still by season. Spring comes when it should come and there is nothing man can do to change that. We get so used to run our lives by time that we forget sometimes that our lives should run by the season. I did not know that until I went to a conference in Los Angeles. One of the workshops I went to was called, "The Season of Change." I was so taken with topic that I went four times to the same workshop. Every season has a place in our lives. We must plan our lives around the season of change. The woman who ran the workshop said, "Every season there must be some change taking place in our lives, and we must ask the Spirit(or)God what to do in each season."

This is the spring season. As I walk around in my neighbourhood and look in my garden that I planted last year, I am amazed at how the energy of love brings back the plants and herbs year after year. Over long winters like the past, plants still survive. When I look at the herbs springing up in the garden, I know there is an energy that makes things grow, and it grows out of that divine love of the universe. I told my neighbour that I saw my herbs and plants bursting from the earth. Man cannot do that, only the power of love could do that. The Spirit of the universe that makes the sun rise and set is that same spirit that wakes us up every morning. The Spirit of the creator is the one that gave us that spirit to sing dance, paint and write. When someone says that they are an artist, my first thinking is, "What kind of artist are you?" Are you the one that works from the five senses, or the one that is in tune with the six senses.

When I started to write about healing, I never thought about it in the way of the senses, or personality and the intuitive inner child. I only wanted to write about the spirit getting sick first and manifesting the sickness through the body by the energy of the soul. That energy makes everything come alive and grow. The energy takes care of us in a way that no one else can. The trees shoot out their buds when it is time to put out its fruits or flowers. No matter where these plants grow, whether inside or outside, that same energy is what makes things grow. If I look at dis-eases in that same way, then I have to ask myself, "Why doesn't that same energy work for the body in the same way?" I believe the reason why things do not work the way man plans it is because we do not stop to listen to the Spirit for its direction, guidance and its protection. There are reasons why the plants and animals do not talk — there are reasons for that. The universe planned it that way. Man does not become animal or plant. Life is not as simple as that, but man has a greater responsibility to talk, think, and ask questions.

Man is a conscious being or soul, with an understanding of the spirit that awakens us inside. We were made to listen and ask questions. No one gets away with anything we do, or say, because someone who is unknown is listening to us talking. I know for myself, I would be thinking about something in silence. Next thing I know, someone in my family, or a friend expresses what I was thinking. Take going to church or the synagogue, I would read some part of the Bible and when I get to church, or the synagogue, the minister or the Rabbi would give his talk on the section of the bible that I read. I would be amazed. I would ask the question, "How did they know that I was reading that part of the bible?" As I started to use the sixth sense, I realized that the Spirit connected us to read that same passage of the Bible. Why then do we not ask the Spirit to teach us how to stay healthy and not get sick. Why does the spirit get sick? The spirit gets sick, because man behaves like we own the spirit by putting it in a box so we do not have to listen or hear what we must do or where to go. We are too busy telling the Spirit what we want and need it to do for us.

I hardly ever heard someone thanking the universe to be here, or for its love. We are always wanting or needing something. The one thing I have learned from the Spirit is not always to desire, or be needy, but be thankful for life. This life is all I have to live out my purpose, when we know what it is. Being an artist is being creative in what our life's purpose is. But lately, I have found out how creativity is related to sexuality. I know that it is the same energy that comes with sexuality, as with creativity. Creativity comes from the sixth sense, and people who use their sixth sense do it from the soul and not from external stimuli.

Some people call the energy, mother nature or God. I call it the Spirit of the universe, and in intimacy, I call it Father. To me, today God is of this world, which is money, power, control and privilege. Healing all the dis-eases will take a lot of that energy. When I think of all those dis-eases, and looking at the suffering of children, especially the one's with cancer, and AIDS, I cry, because I always believe that someone created all these dis-eases for the children, especially the black children from South Africa. I know that the powers of the world know what happened to the children who are dying of AIDS. I know that some day the great big Spirit of the creator who goes to and fro in the earth will reveal the truth about what really happened to the children, and why so many of Africa's children are dying with AIDS.

Balance

When we are off balance, our whole being is out of joint. It is much like having cancer. Last year, I felt I was off balance. My body was tilted to one side. My breathing was so bad when I walked. I started to do yoga to give me back my balance. It is not just something physical, it is psychological, mental, emotional, and most of all spiritual. I was not writing and singing. My spirit was so dampened to the point that I started to get shortness of breath. I started to really pray and talk to the Spirit. I never knew that "Yoga" could make me feel so good inside and out. First thing happened to me is that I lost weight. I did not go on any diet, and I started to read my poem at the university, at a poetry club. I was giving up my purpose. I was not doing what I loved to do, read and talk to people. I got off-track, and yes, it is hard to get back on. I have always had to remind myself about this life and what it consists of, so I can work at it from a spiritual consciousness. Also, I stopped honoring life, and the "Divine." I wanted life to happen my way, not the way of the Spirit. My ego started to take over, by telling me that whatever I want to do is taking too long, so I must give up, and do it exactly the way I was doing before, my way.

Walking on this path of life is a moment to moment journey. Yet, asking for help on this journey, I wanted a quick fix. I wanted everything like yesterday, and when I felt that I was not moving fast enough, I got off-balance. Balance is play, rest, work, and more. But my whole life was off to the point where my spirit got depressed. Balancing life means that I have to ask a lot of questions. 1) Why am I not writing, and what am I afraid of? Why am I off-balance? 2) How do I feel about what I am doing? 3) Am I doing what I love to do? Or do I truly love this life or am I just thinking this is what love is? 4) Am I working from a place of love or from a place of ego, or personality? My spirit was so off-balance to the point where my feet and head felt like I was falling down a steep hill. I started to cry when I asked myself these questions. All the old childhood pain came back in a way that I never looked at it before. The ego brought me back to those places that I thought I had looked at many years ago. I have been looking at my life for a long time. I did not know that I have to live this life, and not just live, but also honor life with the Divine who created this life.

Getting off balance represents a lot of things one needs to look at in their lives. It is not just looking at life, but also being aware of this life in a loving and kind way. The fear I felt was so frightening, that I felt like I was choking. I later found out that I needed to write to my brothers and sisters, whom I put out of my life for nearly twelve years. Here I am, thinking that my life was going the way I wanted it to go, but I left my sisters and brothers out of my life. I stopped writing to them, and yet, I said my life is balanced, and I am a spiritual person, living a spiritual life. How could that be? Yet, I talk about love, and of love. And most of all I talk of wanting that kind of love that looked beyond colours, and what people did. Loving my sisters and brothers had been talk, and not practice, except for my twin sister.

After Papa died and I went home to bury him, I told myself, that I never wanted to see or hear from my two younger sisters and my two younger brothers ever again. I came to Canada in 1967, and in 1969 I went home to bury my mother. Papa was still alive, and my twin sister and I made sure he was financially taken care of. In the last few years of his life, I was the one who sent two hundred Canadian dollars a month to pay someone to make sure that he was clean, eating properly, and having a good place to live. I did not want Papa placed in a nursing home. I wanted him to stay in his own home. My sisters and my youngest brother could not wait for the money to arrive for them to take the money and look after their families, and not Papa. I would not have minded it so much if they had made sure that Papa was being looked after properly. They wanted the money without any of the responsibilities that come with looking after an old person. To them, nothing mattered as long as they got the monthly two hundred and fifty dollars coming to them.

In 1989, Papa died at eighty-six years old. I went to Jamaica to bury him, just like the previous years in the past when I went home and buried Mama. In 1969, I did not have money. I had a bad marriage, and I had just had a baby who was six months old at the time. Twenty years later, I had money to go back to Jamaica and bury Papa. I had just sent the money home to Papa, not knowing that he was sick and in the hospital. When I got to Jamaica, there was no money to bury Papa. My sister, Cherrie took the money and left my twin sister and myself to take care of all the funeral expenses. I was angry, because those two women have never worked a day in their lives. They could have spent some time to care for Papa. All they wanted was just to collect the money. I was a single mother of four children in Canada. I worked hard to raise my children on my own. Life in Canada was not easy unless one sells drug, and even that is hard, because one has to always look behind, and over their shoulders for the police. I have never sent and told them how I was living my life in Canada. I made my bed hard, and I had to sleep in it without letting them know how many nights I went to bed hungry, how many times I was homeless. Yet I have never forgotten Papa. When I was down, meaning I had no money nor a home, I could not send money for Papa, but I knew my twin sister would send the money until I could do so again. I buried Papa, and I came home to Canada. I wrote a few letters and then I stopped writing to them.

In November of 2000, I sat in my favorite chair, and the Spirit spoke so loudly to me, to send one hundred and fifty dollars to my twin sister, who returned home to reside in Jamaica after living in Canada for over thirty years. I listened to the Spirit, and asked a lot of questions to make sure it was the right thing to do. The spirit knew that I did not have a great deal of money to spend over the holiday, but I sent the money. I got a letter shortly after Christmas from my twin sister about my younger brother being homeless, and he had a bad foot, and could hardly walk. He was in need of financial help. The balance that I was off was about my brother. I had worked out all the hurt and anger of the way my parents treated me when I was just a child. What I did not look at was my sisters and brothers. My twin sister and I are the oldest of six children for our father. My mother had five children for her first husband, and he died. My father was the second husband for my mother. The meaning of off-balance in one's life is to make sure that all aspects of our lives is in one accord with the universe.

Man thought that they can create music, dance, and all the forms of creativity — this energy which the creator distributed equally to all of us to create. No one can create anything by themselves without the soul or the spirit. I was so off my mental, emotional, and spiritual balance that I started to put on water weight. The question I asked myself was, "Why is my body holding in the water that I love to drink?" It was not the water — it was my sisters and brothers that I did not write to all these years. I was holding on to their pain of the past.

The Spirit of the universe, the father of all creation spoke to my heart, and let me know that balance is more than work, rest, play, teach, serve and give. It must be an equal part of the whole life. Balance is enlightenment of the soul. A person that is enlightened can do many things in his or her life. While we are enjoying all what we do, we must honor life with "Balance." After I wrote to my brothers and sisters, I felt all the love and joy come back to my soul.

Choice

Choice is my divine teacher. I did not know about choice until I read Iyanla Vanzant's book, "One Day When My Soul Just Opened Up." I have been writing about choosing but not about choice, in the way Iyanla set it out in her book, so that I could understand what I was writing about. Choice is divine, and when I honor myself with choice, I am also divinely seeking help for the choices I made, so that the Spirit of the universe will guide with its wisdom. Here I am thinking that I know everything, but I did not know anything. My addiction is money, I do not know how to spend it wisely. I was always telling my friend about the job or the money before I got it in my hand. I was not making wise choices. I was not divinely guided on how to spend money. When I was a little girl, I worked hard for money, and as soon as I got the money, my father would take it from me and give it to my twin sister. Looking back now, I realized that it was not the money, it was me. I needed to know how to ask for help when it came to money in my life.

Choice is one of the major challenges today, because people do not want to take responsibility for their action so they are afraid to make a choice. Choice is the alternative for change. Choice is free will, and free will means that I am free to make divinely guided changes in my life that are in agreement with the universal Spirit. Choice teaches me to listen to my soul and heart, to travel on the right path, to travel on in this life.

When I was a little girl, I had to made choices that affected my life until this day. I wanted to know God. I was five years old, and because of that choice that I made back then, I learned to love with my whole heart, and to care about people. When I turned eleven years old, I met an older girl who said she loved me. I mean that she said that she really loved me. She wanted to have sex with me. I had no one to talk to, but my best friend whom I called, "The shadow." I told "the shadow" about the woman who said she loved me. I talked to the Spirit or I prayed as I always do, and she left me alone. Over the years, I met a lot of women in Canada who said that they loved me or wanted me to be their lover. I have always thought that people make choices in their lives. When I heard homosexual people say that they are born like that, wanting the same sex for their lover, it made me angry, because I am a twin and even twins they said, one will become homosexual. I made a choice not to have sex with the same person like myself, since I was eleven years old. Homosexually is a spirit and it is the spirit of choice that one makes that determines how one wants to live his or her life.

I told my daughter the other day that there is no evil and there is no satan. Satan or evil is the choice that people make in their lives. People do not speak up and say what they need or want. They just go along with what is going on. Society's life is fashionable. We go with the trend and every year we have to buy new trends. We look like the neighbour down the street.

Choice is our teacher, if we are willing to listen to the teacher inside of us, but most of the time we are too afraid to listen to the Spirit. So we listen to the self that is talking and we accepted the temptation, because of the choice we refused to make and to listen to. Please do not tell me that mother nature made mistakes with your birth. I made a choice that I have to live with for the rest of my life on planet earth. I went back to my ex-husband and

I knew that it was the wrong thing to do, but I was too afraid to walk away, and I got my son who cannot cope with life. From the day I said I was pregnant, he abused me until the day my son was born. I made a choice and it was not divinely guided. I cried so loudly one day, that I heard a voice say, "Long term challenges will be your life with your son." I just stopped crying and accepted the consequences of the choices I made so long ago when I was afraid of living in Toronto alone. Choice will give you or me a place of harmony, where peace of mind, and of heart teach us to truly trust this life that is given to us to honor the creator of the universe. Choice gives us the courage to grow and the power to be gentle, loving, and kind. Our purpose is to make change or choose the alternative so we can grow to the end of our days on this earth.

Education

Healing of the mind is not education. Education, if it is not from the heart and soul, is not knowledge. Knowledge is learning, but without the soul or the spirit involved, it is not knowledge. I have a daughter who never stopped going to school, and still did not know what she wanted to do — until one day she took a course in floral arrangement and loved it. Then she decided to go and learn about plants and gardening. She loved that too. She is now in university taking geography and loving it. That is what education is all about — doing what you love to do.

There is nothing wrong with school, but school must be about life, because that is where we learn to ask for guidance, protection and direction. We need to learn and find out why man is on earth. What is man's purpose on earth? It is not going to university for four or seven years and saying I am this or that, and because I am a doctor in this or that I know. Knowing is when the universe is involved in our lives, and becoming directors of our lives. I have learned that man is the actor, and the universe is the producer and director of all of us, so man has no claim to education. Just because we went to educational institutions and spent four to seven years, and we received this paper that said we have studied in this field, that does not mean this is our purpose or our calling.

Education is a calling to learn, and to be at a higher level in our spirit. Our minds and hearts are in accord with the Spirit, not just what some man told us to read and write about in our life. Institutional learning is man-made, and it was created by the establishment in our society to separate people from each other. That is how the class system came into being. It was never the plan of the Spirit of the father, creator of the universe to put up walls of separation between each other. That is the power and control of man. Learning must come from the soul, mind, and heart. The true meaning of education is about life and learning. Man has become so mechanical today, we have become very lazy in dealing with each other. We do not read for fun, it is all about money. The systems are designed in a way so that we do not think for ourselves. If I did not give away someone else's money, I would not think twice of becoming a machine like the rest of the society and disrespecting true art in the process.

Man's thoughts are of everything else except how to take care of the body which is the house for the spirit. Education is knowing how to take care of the spirit and the body, so that no dis-eases can take hold of the spirit. Healing is being able to take care of the body, mind and spirit.

"Father, yesterday as I was reading over the piece that I wrote about my childhood, I couldn't believe that I handed over my life to people that cannot take care of themselves, much less to manage my life for me. Please forgive me for thinking that anyone outside of myself can manage my life better than me. What I was doing was looking for the mother and father that I never had. Thank you for reminding of the awareness that only you can manage my life for me. I always want someone to do it for me. I couldn't believe I could do such a thing until you reminded me that I am the only one who can do it the way you wanted it done. Thank you, Father for your love and the understanding of your love."

Chapter 4

Awareness

Awareness is the consciousness of the spirit of the soul that connects to the source, which is the Spirit of the universe, the creator of heaven and earth. There is a spirit that man calls holy, which goes back and forth throughout the earth. That is the creator's spokesperson. It is a spirit that one cannot see with the real eyes, but only through the heart. By doing so, one has to listen to one's heart, because that is where the soul of man or the spirit of man resides. I found out that when I am angry or fearful of something, I push my feelings away. Where I really push my feelings away is in the subconscious and only the Spirit of the creator of the universe can summon it to the consciousness.

Awareness means understanding up front in our minds so that our emotions can take hold of whatever it is we can deal with. For a long time, I did not know how this spirit worked in my life. I wanted to know God since I was a little girl of five years old. As I grew older and hungrier, the yearning to know got louder in my soul for wanting to know the Spirit of the creator. The noise in my heart and head was so loud that I went on a search for answers outside of myself, because I thought that I should look outside to the people who claimed that they knew the answers. The more I searched outside of myself, the more challenges I faced. My search got more difficult because I was looking outside of myself for the answer.

Awareness! Every time I think about the outside of myself, I wondered if people knew what was best for me. Every time I think about this word, *awareness*, I have to sit and get my thoughts together and ask a lot of questions. And the search started all over again in my soul. The question was, "What is awareness?" At first I thought it was what I perceived in my mind, and what I felt inside. The dictionary said, *It's conscious; informed; as, he is well aware of one's shortcomings.*

Awareness to me is the gut feeling that one feels inside that stops one in their tracks to let them pay attention to what is going on in their lives. When I was listening to the outsider, I didn't hear what was going on inside of me. I was too busy with the outsider to listen because they knew what was best for me. It was not until I was beaten by my ex-husband and ended up in hospital. I realized that it was the outsider talking for me — not the insider which is the Spirit of the creator of my soul. There will be people who know or think they know what is best for me or for you. From time immemorial, there were always people who think they are the one hearing from God and no one else, and the only way they think so is because most of us are afraid to pay attention to our "insider." The fact is, if we listen to what is being said, we will have to respond and make changes and people are afraid of change. Awareness is the ability to recognize the spirit of the universe in action, truth and knowledge. To put it another way, intuitive feeling is of the heart in the soul, and with that awareness, we can listen for guidance on how to make better choices, because it is the path of true judgment and right living. Awareness occurs when the eyes and heart are open to receiving the Spirit, so that one can learn how to listen to what is going on around and inside of oneself. Awareness is also the understanding of the knowledge of the Spirit of the creator of the universe that allows man to dream dreams and gives man the ability to bring those dreams into focus on the purpose of why each and everyone of us is here on planet earth. No one on earth knows more than each other. We think otherwise, however, because man is conditioned from generation to generation to control and brainwash each other to the point that most people are too afraid to think for themselves. I too was taking that path until one day when I got sick with asthma and I had to start paying attention to my health.

Awareness is the spirit of knowing that I am safe in the love and energy of the creator of the universe. And knowing how to pray to the Spirit or in the circle of the creator of love on the inside of the heart. When I was growing up in my little village, and going around telling everyone who would listen to me that I wanted to know God and that I would serve God when I grew up, I thought it was just to get people angry at me. The villagers used to really get angry at me for saying that to them. In my heart as a little girl, I knew that was what I really wanted to do with my life — to love the lord, the creator of heaven and earth, the Spirit of the universe. I would pray or talk with the Spirit. The people in the village wanted to know if the Spirit talked. I told them yes. I was only a little girl, and all through those years living in the village of Winchester, that was my longing. When I became a teenager, I ran away from home but I still had that wanting and I still had that knowing the Spirit of the universe which today everyone calls God. I have never stopped yearning to know in spite of all the hardship and the challenges I have faced and been through. I still yearn to grow and know more. Awareness is not only spiritual, it is also mental, emotional and psychological. To be able to grasp all this awareness in the heart and soul, one has to be so in tune with life and oneself to process all this spiritual knowing. It was a hard lesson for me to learn. That wanting to know and knowing takes a lot of time and energy to learn and to practise. It was not just talking and telling the people what I want to do, it was doing what I wanted to do and working out what my purpose in this life is all about. It is allowing the spirit to work from your heart, so that the soul can learn what its purpose is on earth. Awareness gives one the ability to go inside and pull the heart and soul together so that the mind has no choice but to listen and learn and practise. It is a place where only you alone can go. I call that life and place a journey into the unknown.

Awareness will take us where no one else can go for us. It goes into the depth of the soul where the soul finds peace, joy and love for the universe and for human beings on earth. It was then that I found out that just wanting to know is not enough for my life, but knowing is a different thing because I started to practise what I knew in spite of the outsiders and their noise.

Chapter 5

Ancestors

Ancestors- who are these people? Were they killers? Did they have hatred in their hearts? Did they help others? Did they love themselves? Were they wealthy? Were they kind, truthful and loving? Did they believe in God or the creator. Were they religious, or spiritual? Did they work the land? I do not know them, but I hope they were positive in what they did and said. I know that mixed culture.

November 26, 1968 was a Thursday, very much like today. It was damp, cold and overcast. I was not expecting the baby until the end of the month or the beginning of December. I had already had three girls, but one never knew what to expect when having a baby. Sometimes, it could come early, sometimes late, but only Mother nature and the universal Spirit know what they are doing.

When I was pregnant with my first daughter, I was so sick, but not only sick. I was afraid of pain and dying. I did not want any more children, but when my second daughter was born, the same thing happened to me — the fear of pain almost killed me. Yet, I had another daughter, but this time having the third girl was a breeze. She was even born at home, unlike the first two. They were born at the hospital. The doctor did not want to take any chances with my life.

I was born in Jamaica, in the West Indies. When I first found out that I was pregnant here in Canada, I knew that it was a boy, because I fainted, and with the girls I knew that they were girls too. If you live in the five senses world, your heart is close to the spirit of knowing, and the spirit knows and speaks. I always hear most of the time what the Spirit is saying to me, but I was too afraid of George, my ex-husband. So I went along with what George wanted, because of fear of speaking out about what I wanted, and the fear of being beaten for speaking out. When I first found out that I was pregnant, I was the one who told the doctor that I was going to have a baby, and that it was a boy. He looked at me like I was crazy. The doctor even laughed in my face. Then he bet me five hundred dollars, but I would not get the money until the baby was born. If it was today, I would have taken the bet. Back then I did not understand what was going on. So I let him have his laugh. One thing I knew for sure I was going to have a baby in the fall, and it was a boy. I told the doctor that he will see, and that he would not be laughing then.

In the early morning of November 26, 1968 I started to have labour pains on and off all day. My water broke around six p.m. the same day, and my so-called husband and my friend took me to the hospital. To be precise, "Doctor's Hospital." For the next four days, I was in pain. That baby would not budge until Saturday, November 30, at 12.30 p.m. when the doctor came to see one of his other patients. That was when he found out that I was there since Thursday. No one had bothered to call and let him know that I was in the hospital. I had delivered a baby boy. It happened just the way I had told him since the first time I met him in his office. The reason why I am writing about my son is because he has something to do with my thoughts about ancestors.

My mother was born on a Saturday, a long time ago. I did not know my maternal grandmother. My grandmother died before I was born. She died when my mother was five years old. I did not know anything about her because my mother never talked about her. I did not even know her name. It was like my mother never had a mother. Then there was my paternal grandfather and my mother's father, only my father's mother was alive when my sister and I were born. If they were still alive, I would not have known them, because I was born far away from where my grandmother was living at the time. My father said that his mother knew my twin sister, my brother and I. I did not remember her. We were still too young and my brother was a baby. I do not know who these people were. I know my maternal grandmother was part Indian, part Spanish. For instance, a few months ago, I went to a computer store downtown Toronto and one of the employees was a Spanish-speaking man who came up to me and started to speak in Spanish. I answered him in French. I was told that he was speaking Spanish to me. I had forgotten that my mother spoke Spanish. The same with my father speaking German. My father's mother was German and whatever else mixed in with the German and black. My paternal grandfather was from North Africa.

The ancestors of yesteryear have a lot to do with what happens to our lives. If we do not sit down and ask the Spirit of the universe, creator of heaven and earth who were these people, we could be constantly going around in circles. I was born in Jamaica, but these people who preceded me came from some place else. They had gone through a lot of their own challenges in their lives. The black people who ended up in Jamaica came from Africa via the slave trade. The Germans who ended up in Jamaica were there for another reason and the same for others such as the Spanish and French and also the Indian. I wanted to know who these people were because all I ever knew and saw about these people were in my dreams.

Why was my son born on the day my mother was born? What significance does this have on me and my son? The people that have gone on before us play a role in our daily lives. I keep asking the Spirit about these who supposedly were my ancestors. Somewhere in my subconscious, I see myself as they see me. I feel how they feel, and sometimes I look at my children one by one and want to know, "Is anyone of my children my great grandmother?" Then I wanted to know if I am one of them. Sometimes, I feel that I belong to all these ancestors who are part of my life. The people that are on planet earth do not realize that we are all one. We were all born on this earth, and even though we are trying to create man, I do not believe man will be able to create himself. I have been searching myself, looking for my ancestors in my children and now my grand-children and hoping that I can learn something about who I am and therefore pass it on to them.

Jamaica is located near Cuba, and Cuba is a Spanish-speaking country. Jamaica was also Spanish before the French and then the English came and took it over. Then all the others came in and became part of this beautiful island where it is hot all year round except when it rains. The spirit of the ancestors is here with us, and if we do not stop and reflect on who these people were, we would never be whole. It is like not paying attention to the Spirit of the creator of the universe. Our life would consist of aimless wanderings in the wilderness. Until my father died, I never missed a day when I dreamt of seeing my mother. Then my father died and now I hardly ever dream of my mother.

My mother became my daughter. I had to take care of my mother since I was seven years old until I was almost twelve years old. My mother died when I was twenty-four years old. She would appear in my dreams and I would know what was going on, and all that stopped when my father died. Before my mother died, there was always some spirit with me. I have always felt protected, because I wanted to know the Spirit of the Creator of heaven and earth. I have never thought it was the ancestors of my mother and father. I always thought that it was the Holy Spirit that guided, directed and protected me. In 1986, my son was in and out of mad houses. He had five nervous breakdowns and I could not understand what was going on. I found myself asking the creator why history was repeating itself again? Suddenly, I thought of my mother who had the same fate, and I had to be strong to pick up the pieces of her life, my own and my sisters' and brothers'. I had so many questions about who these people were. They were from the past, could I deal with my son like I dealt with my mother? I was older and stronger, but I did not know if I could handle madness like I did when I was seven. Now I was in my late thirties and early forties.

One day I met a friend of mine at the train station, and I was telling him about my son who was in the mad house. Right away he took my hand and off we went to St. Michael Catholic church. He was Catholic and I was not but went along with him. I did not care — I just knew that no matter where I am praying, the Spirit of the Creator would be there to show me how to change my circumstances if my heart was in the right place. We arrived at the church, went in and knelt down as they do in the Catholic church on the bench. He grabbed my hand and looked in my eyes and said to me, "First, you must pray for the ancestors, because you and I do not know what they were feeling when they departed from this life. So, let us ask the father, the creator of the universe to guide their spirits with love to a peaceful place, where they will find rest for themselves." I was shocked to learn all this. "Father," I said, "I am asking to guide my ancestors to a place of peace and love so that my son can be healed in his mind and body, and most of all, in his spirit. Father, my son's spirit is sick, and his sickness is manifested in his mind." I prayed like this for one whole hour, then he prayed like that for another half an hour. I started to cry, because I could not believe that the ancestors had something to do with my son's life. After we finished praying, we sat in quietness for what seemed like eternity. I never spoke to him — he never spoke to me. We just sat in silence. That day I went home with respect and lots of love in my heart for my friend, and renewed faith, and truth for the creator of the universe. Did the Father hear us that day? Yes! As I prayed for the ancestors first, my son started to feel better and do better in his mind. That was fifteen years ago. I had forgotten all about that until now.

I am now facing my son and his breathing problems like I did with my mother. In the old testament, Zechariah chapter one, and verses three to six, the Lord was asking question about the fathers of old and the prophets. The lord wanted to know what your father of old did. They did not listen to the prophet. The creator was talking about Israel and Judah. Their forefathers never listen to the prophet when they talked and warned about the God of Israel. The Lord said, "If you turn to me, I will turn to you, but did they listen?" That goes for me. When my mother told me not marry George, I told her to mind her own business. What I was facing now was worse than what my mother was saying to me so long ago. The ancestors have a place in our lives. If we as people do not listen to the Spirit of the father, there will always be negative consequences for the choices we have made. What I did not know then, was that in this life there is a bigger picture to take into consideration, and the decision that I made would have affected others in our lives.

The people in our lives are affected no matter what we do. My mother had a nervous breakdown. Now my son faces the same thing, but it was not just on my side of the family. George's side of the family too, had madness in their lives. I should have listened to my mother — she knew something that I did not know that was hidden from me. And by the time I found out, it was too late. My friend told me that it was not too late — God the father of the universe would help me, and show me what to do as I prayed for the ancestors first. After my son started to make a come-back to living his life, I had stopped praying for the spirit of the ancestors. I thought that he was okay, but now I have to start all over again because his lungs are malfunctioning.

Healing

I know now for sure that it is really the spirit of man that really is in need of healing. The ancestors that have gone on before cannot be in the flesh, but in the spirit. As I said before, my son is now battling for his lungs to be well so that he can breathe without pain. That was my mother's challenge, fighting for her lungs, not just my mother, but also my cousin and uncle. Somewhere in the broader scheme of things, the ancestors have something to do with us. The spirits of these people hang around us, and I believe that as humans who are on earth, we have to talk to our spirit, that we do not want what our ancestors had when they were alive. What I did was, I told my spirit that I do not want my mother's dis-ease, no lung malfunction, and no depression. My mother was always sick when I was a little girl with everyone taking care of her. One day my dad found out that my mother had TB. At the time, everyone was shocked, but looking back now, yes! she made herself sick, so that everyone would pay for her not having a mother. Her mother died when she was five years old, and I am sure that the people who raised her, abused her. She was a bright and intelligent woman, and even though she had only a grade three education, she could do so many things out of her imagination. She could sing, sew, and memorize poems. And she was a great storyteller. She taught all her children how to sing. We had a choir in our home. Yet, with all that talent, she used them in a negative way by complaining about her not having a mother.

My mother spent all her waking moments looking for her mother. She prayed, yet her mother did not come, so I became her mother. What my mother needed to do was to ask God for help. I had to ask the Father, the creator for help — to come and be the mother and father I did not have. I was doing the same thing like my mother. Especially looking for the dad I did not have when I was a little girl. What she needed to do was ask for help from the universe(God) so that she could be healed from the past of not having a mother. I was going to be in my mother's shadow. I started to behave like her, wanting someone to take care of me — I felt sorry for myself. Even though I was praying, I was doing what mammy did until one day I found myself dying, and I took a long look at me.

Once, I looked at me in the mirror, and I started to cry and ask the question, "Mary, why are you living like your mother?" I would get so sad and depressed if things or life did not go my way. I was so caught up in religion that I could not see that my life was like my mother's. Here is my son now taking on my mother's spirit, feeling sorry for himself. I always believed that only selfish people become mad. I believe that when I did not get what I wanted, I got depressed. My son had no confidence in himself, that was why he wanted her dis-ease. I found out that this kind of behavior is from the ancestors. I told myself I did not want to be like the ancestors, I do not want their sickness and their diseases. Did I just come up with this overnight? No, I was always sad — this sadness always came over me, and I didn't know why. "Why am I so sad," I would say to myself? "Or this feeling of sorrow." I would read the bible and pray. I knew that my focus was to know God, so why was I feeling such sorrow and sadness, especially when I turned thirty. I thought it was a hormonal thing, so I went to a doctor, and I was healthy. Was it all in my head? I now know it was stuff that I buried deep down in my subconscious and I was not dealing with the past. Without dealing with the past, the present, and future are blurred, and all we do is travel in circles. I went on a quest to help myself and to heal myself. I did not want to go and talk to anyone about my past, so that they could use me as a study case and write a book about me and make millions of dollars, when I still have the problem.

Self-help Books

There are millions of self-help books on the market today, telling us how to, yet millions of people are still lost. The self-help books are like the bible. Billions of copies of the bible are sold each year, yet people are so religious, excluding spirituality. We are inundated with all kinds of self-help books along with the bible. But unless we put what we read into practice, we are no where. There is a saying that we must practise what we preach. If we just read and talk about what we read, we are not going any place. It takes time to mentally and emotionally process what we read and apply it to our lives. Another thing that is wrong with some of the self-help books are the people who write them. Most of the people only write the books because they have a degree in psychology, and they think they know human nature.

Self-help books — what's wrong with them, nothing — if they are being used in a manner where people can teach themselves. I love to read, and study and learn, and when I have a problem to deal with, I go looking for help in books. I started to search for the real Mary Wright. I knew that she needed help, and I also knew that no one could help her but me. Yes, all my life I wanted to know the Father and the creator of the whole earth, the creator of the universe. I wanted to know, but I could not know until I cleaned up my life and got rid of the sadness that lay beneath my soul. Sometimes I would pray all night but nothing happened, because I was not getting to the depth of the soul. Religion does not heal the soul. Only the Spirit of the father, the creator of the universe.

It is a mental, emotional and spiritual place that I needed to go, and the only way I could do that is by asking for help, and that help cometh from the Lord which made heaven and earth. I did not know that it was a daily working at. I started working out some deep-rooted pain of sadness in my blood from the ancestors who have passed on before.

The spirit of life is in our blood. I really believe that and only the Spirit of the universe can help us to cleanse the blood. My mother had everything wrong with her because she did not know how to work out the deep-rooted fear, anger, shame and sadness that she had to live with all her life. I could have ended up like her. I was on my way by the time I was twenty-seven years old and living in Canada, because that was what I was taught since I was two years old. I could sense my mother's fear of my father. How could someone lay their hand on someone and all their pain and fear go away? Fear and anger are like cancer — it goes in to remission, and as something triggers it, it is back again. The only way cancer will ever heal, is if people work at it every day, because it is in the blood, and the spirit of any man is in the blood, which is life. Praying or talking to the creator who knows where the spirit lies, is good, but we need more than just praying. We need to take action by finding out how we can cleanse the spirit.

I have always wondered what would have happened to me when I started to behave like my mother — if I never got a hold of my life and really begin to ask questions. I remember I would get up out of bed and walk from 1 am to 3 am in the morning asking for help for my life. I did not know what my real purpose was at the time. I was confused, not knowing where I was going. I was just lost in my soul. I wanted to know the God of the universe — I was determined to find out what my life's purpose was. At the time, I had four small children to take care of, and I did not want to be like my mother, making my oldest daughter become my mother. I saw history was going to repeat itself, and told myself in those early morning walks and talking to the Spirit of the father about my life and that I needed help, and to help me so that I did not become my mother. My ex-husband left me with four children like my father left my mother. My father was around, but only for my twin sister. My mother did not have a mother, but she had a father who loved her until he remarried. When her father rejected her for his second wife, my mother was lost, and she spent the rest of her life feeling sorry for herself. Today, they call it the "Poor me syndrome." Feeling that no one loved her, she made herself sick, so she would be taken care of. I know now that my mother felt that the only person in this world she needed to love was herself. I can love you the way you are. I needed to be loved. I had to learn that hard lesson before I ended up like my mother. I know she could have lived as long as my father.

My father lived for twenty years longer than my mother. He died when he was eighty-six years old. Mama wanted to be healed on her terms, not on God terms. I was young, but I told my mama to go back to the city and let Papa stay in the country. He was happy in Winchester in St. Thomas, Jamaica. Papa belonged there, Mama did not, not in that rainy place, but she was too afraid to leave.

Why I am writing about my parents and myself is to show that it is the spirit that gets sick first. It is the spirit that needs to be healed first, and no matter how many doctors we go to, the ancestors have a strong hold on us until we recognize that. If not, we die with their sickness and dis-ease. Mama had everything wrong with her. You name it, my mama had it, only because that little girl inside of this woman did not grow up. Mama could see and feel things about people. The villagers used to call her "Goat Mouth," meaning anything that was going to happen to anyone in the village, my mama would know and warn the villagers. She stopped people from going to jail for drugs, from committing murder, or breaking into other villager's houses, but she could not save herself, because it was easier to tell others what to do, than to do it for herself — doing it for one's self is harder. Mama was also afraid of herself too. I watched her save my brother from being killed by a truck. She was always warning others what was going to happen and what will happen if they went some place or did something. No one could fool my mother, and the same went for my Papa too. These two people were so intuitive, but they never really did anything with the gift that was given to them for themselves, but used the gifts to help others. I was doing the same thing too. First, the gifts or gift that one feels that the creator gave to them should be first sorted out, and then its purpose discovered. Then, one should seek direction as to what way one may use the gift and for whom. People that did not even like my mother liked to be near her — the same with my father. Wherever they were, people listened to their advice and how and where to live and where to work. What those two needed was a real spiritual healing in their souls. Their souls needed to learn what they came to earth to learn, but there was no one to teach them. I was their teacher for a while, but they were always shipping me off like a parcel to live with strangers who did not know who they were. They were just children like my parents, but off I went to share the blessing of the gifts that I was born with — with these strangers.

Some of these strangers were so damaged from their past, it was hard to break through the walls that they put up in their souls. The betrayal, rejection, and abandonment were hard for a lot of the people that my parents sent me to live with. At the time, all they wanted from me was to collect other people's money on their behalf. All of the people that I went to live with including my mother's sister, were very wealthy in land. Having a lot of acres of land when I was a little girl was money and power. Lots of people worked for these people, even though they could not read or write. I read for them, wrote for them, and kept their books for them. My allowances each week went to my parents. They always had food when I was away.

"The earth is the Lord's and the fulness thereof"

The earth belongs to the creator of the universe — the Spirit that dwells in all of man on the earth. No man can ever own the earth, it belongs to the lord. I found it hard sometimes to watch people fighting over land that they will never own and when they die, leave it all behind. Yet we fight, and we even create war thinking we own something. All of mankind came to this earth and we have to leave it behind some day, and I believe that is why man wants to destroy the earth and all that is in it, but it is impossible for that to happen. The creator will not let that happen. They have gone to the moon, and space, and even built a space station. "Man said, they have moon stone, now they want the sun stone." Now they want to go to the heaven — man has such a big ego. They are like my parents helping everyone instead of themselves. Man wants power and control over others. No matter how many wars are fought on this earth, man will die, but the earth remaineth — that is what I really believe right now. The earth is in need of a spiritual healing, but the only way that can happen, man has to find out what their purpose is. The earth will heal itself.

Everywhere I go, there is talk about the water being polluted, so is the earth and the air that we breathe. What makes the earth polluted, man. Man wants power and control, but until we recognize that no one can control the earth or the universe, the disease and sickness is here to stay. Only the Spirit of the creator knows what is going on. There are so many wars fought for the earth, yet no man owns the earth as yet and never will. The universal Spirit of the father which is creator of the heaven and earth will heal all things in its own time. I know that the spirit will heal itself one day, but in the meantime man's heart, and soul needs renewal of the right spirit so that their hearts can become flesh.

When I started to write this paper on healing, I started out with lots of question about dis-ease. One of the main ones is heart, cancer, AIDS, and diabetes. Billions of dollars have been spent on these dis-eases, and there are no cures, and there will not be cures until the creator takes back full control of the earth. All the great doctors and scientists that have been on earth have tried to find cures, and to heal man with their man-made wisdom, knowledge, and their so-called understanding. Yet, they have not got rid off dis-ease yet. My mother had TB — no man could heal my mother but the Spirit of the creator that I used to pray and talk to at night and day to heal my mother. Man cannot get the body well until the spirit of the soul is healed, because wellness comes from the Spirit of the soul which is the Lord. My mother told my father she would like to see me become a doctor, because I have healing in my hand and a pure heart, and I would help people to find themselves. What she really meant to say at the time was that I have healing in my soul, or my purpose in this life is to help others by being a servant of God. She said that I have the gift of healing, that people who have the gift of healing must work from a religious venue. I did not understand at the time what she meant — all I knew was I wanted to know God and I started to pray and fast for help for the villagers, and if they were sick, I prayed for healing for them and they would be healed. I always prayed for my mother when she had TB. As long as I was there in Jamaica, my mother was safe, because she knew I would be there for her. My mother gave up when I came to Canada. I had forgotten that I was her lifeline to living since I was seven year old. When I came to Canada, I still wanted to be in a religious setting to serve God.

If there was a Jesus as people claimed there was in the bible, he did not build some big organization with everyone jockeying for power and control. Jesus could teach us human beings in the twenty-first century, (that the kingdom of God) the Spirit of the father the creator of heaven and earth lives in man. Wherever man goes, the spirit goes with him or her. I believe that the only way real healing can take place is if we human beings are connected to the source, which is the Spirit of the creator. That is the Divine law. When we are connected, only then can man lead and teach each other how to be connected, and to know what the truth of God the father is. Only then the sick will be healed, and the blind eyes will see and ears will be open — all human beings will be made whole.

Everything that looks wrong outside of us really comes from the inside of our soul. The earth is made so that all men can live and learn how the spirit of truth lives in all of us which allows even the grass to grow and herbs for medicine to heal the body through the spirit. I believe that if men were connected to the source which is the Divine law, man would not have to worry about food, dis-ease and sickness. The spirit would be clean, and so would be the body.

Human-Race

The only race on earth is the human-race. All I ever hear today is the race card playing back and forth. Here we are telling each other about white race, black race yellow and red race. I have never seen or heard such an illusion in my whole life. What does colour and culture have to do with race? There are no black or white races, just colours and cultures on this earth. I know that one day all of us who sat back and watched people fight about colour, and said nothing, will have to give an account of our omission. They just went along with the race-playing card — that included me. Sometimes I watched white people believing that being white is a passport to use and abuse others, and I also look at black people screaming about because they are black — that is why this or that is happening to them. I refuse to take that way out, because taking that attitude will either send me to prison or let me feel so hopeless that I end up in the mad house. People, it is not about colour — it has never been, it is about equality, money, power and control. It is not about economics, and class systems — where one lives, how much money one has, where one went to school and who are their parents. In the broader scheme of things, it is about the class system that we all grew up with. The Spirit of the father does not see colour, it sees the heart and soul of all men.

Fear is the number one killer of the spirit of the soul. When fear takes over, man sees colour. We blame each other for what is wrong in our life. Only man creates colour, not the Spirit. If race is part of the creator's plan as man said, all black people would have died out. The white man has been trying to kill off black people for so long, but we are still here. It is fear of each other why we talk about races, because it makes us feel good about ourselves. Also, the power and the establishment of society create fear between people for so long, and this fear is to keep each other apart, because if we are all on the playing field, we will be equal to everyone. There are no races on earth, only people (human beings).

Chapter 6

Dis-Ease

Dis-ease, as I know it, has two parts to the life: physical and the spiritual. It is of the mind and spirit. I understand what it means to be dies-eased, but here is what The *Winston Canadian Dictionary* said about Dis-ease. It is a disorder of mind, or body marked by definite symptoms, illness, sickness and any particular instances or kinds of, such as heart dis-ease. This is what the dictionary defined. So I went a little farther as I meditated and prayed about what I wanted to write about, in terms of dis-ease and healing. I then looked up the word "Ease."

Ease:
1) Freedom from pain, labour, worry, trouble, etc.; as ease of body and mind; (2) naturalness as ease manner; -VT (eased) easing free from pain, anxiety, stress etc. give relief to as, medicine to ease the pain; good news ease the mind (3) to loose anything tight as to ease a band; also, to move, gentle, to ease a stretcher into an ambulance, don't-ease.

Cancer

Cancer, what is it? Where did it come from? Why is there no cure, or why can't man find the cure for cancer? I can tell you why, because treating cancer is a money-making business. For the last ten years, I have been wondering what the root cause of cancer is. Is it some thing in the food that we eat, or is it the water that we use for drinking? What is going on in the body that we ourselves as people cannot cure? Another thing I have been doing is asking my friends who are still working as nurses, where cancer came from, and what does it look like? Two weeks ago, I was talking to my friend who is a nurse, who everytime she calls me is to inform me once again of someone we know who died of breast cancer. I asked her if cancer was like boils? She said, "Yes, they are always talking about lumps in the breast." I then said to her, "It must be those lumps that sometime is under the arm pit, or on the groin between the legs, near the vagina that turn inside of the body and get into the blood." She said, "Yes, something like that."

In the seventies, I used to work as a homemaker for home care. One assignment I had at the time was a man in Unionville on a farm. In those days, I had to stay four hours at one place. Looking back now, I believe the doctor sent the man home to die. One day the nurse was late in coming so I changed the dressing for him. What I saw was a big lump on his neck spewing out that puss. It smelled so badly, and he was in so much pain. That was my first look at cancer in Canada, but I have seen those big lumps (we call boils) on people's neck in Jamaica when I was a little girl. My mother and father had those lumps. I remember my father had a big one and he used to dress it himself. I remember my father telling me that if I did not clean the inside of the body, those lumps would kill me, because they have poison in them. The puss is poison, if it gets into the blood.

Cancer, I believe, is those lumps that people develop. When I was a child, back then people called the lump boils. Every six months when my siblings and I were young, we would get our blood purged with all kinds of bitter bark. After all that purging, we would get six months of tonic to rebuild the body, as my father insisted. Also, we never ate a lot of red meat, mostly fish, vegetables, and fruit. My friend said the cancer turned inside instead out through the skin. I asked my sister the same question about the lump that Papa used to have on his neck and armpit. She said that it was what we now call Cancer. She then went on to describe some as having roots. I told her that the lump (boil) I knew of, some of them had roots, but never killed anyone. She said that people were not as busy and people were purging the body and there was good water to drink, and not so much toxin in the water, food, and air. Another thing I remembered when I was a child, drinking water was encouraged, even babies had to drink lots and lots of water.

Cancers and tumors are North America's way of manipulating people's minds so that they do not know what this "lump" is all about and that we do not think about our bodies. Most of us pay so much attention to how we look on the outside, so while we pay attention to how we look outside, the inside suffers with all kinds of lumps (boils), and by the time we realize something is wrong, the boil toxin is in our blood and finds its way into all parts of our inner organs. Papa was right in purging our blood and not allowing us to eat a lot of red meat, and feed us herbs in drinks to keep us healthy. My father was a spiritual man, and he did not believe in God like we do today. He believed that the whole body needed purging including the mind, soul, and body.

Dis-eases, like Cancer, AIDS, TB, Diabetes, etc., are not just of the mind, they are of the spirit — they manifest through the body, because the spirit cannot be seen. The spirit manifests itself in thoughts, which is the mind and feelings. The spirit of the soul gets sick first, usually when these dis-eases come upon us. It is a wake-up call for us to pay attention to something that is going on in our lives, or around us, that you or I need to be aware of, and to ask for help from the Spirit. The body is where you and I learn our lessons through the soul. Dis-eases are our lessons to learn so that we are kept in accord with the Spirit of the "Divine law." That is true, but if we do not pay attention to what is going on in our lives, that is when the spiritual law will work out its purpose in our lives, by allowing things to happen to us, so that we pay attention. Most of us in North America only think about the spirit when we are in trouble and are in need of help. There is a Divine law like there are physical laws. Most of us only pay attention to physical laws, but there are more to our lives than just paying attention to the law that man set up about the ten commandments. Even the Ten Commandments are spiritual laws, not physical ones.

Last season, I got a call from my oldest daughter about my son having lung cancer or possibly, general cancer. I, for the first time did not panic about it. My first question was, "Spirit of the father, what are you trying to say to me? I know that it's not mine to handle, but because I am his mother, I think you want me to know something isn't right in my life." I used to be a "poor me" person. Why is all this happening to me? It is always "Why me," and I would be screaming and telling all my friends about what is going on in my life. I learned that I should talk to the Spirit of the father, creator of the universe and not to my friend right away. I learned the "poor me" syndrome during my childhood from my mother who was always feeling sorry for herself. All this childhood dis-ease is of the heart and spirit, and the only way you or I can deal with this feeling of "poor me" is when it manifests itself in the body, not even the mind. I believe that the soul is in the bottom of the heart. Through the mind is how we know, feel and think for ourselves. The heart is the seat of the soul. We think through the mind, we know what the heart is saying to us only through feeling.

Another thing I found out lately is that our thoughts have to be in tune with our heart so that you or I will know what is being said to us through our hearts and mind. But if we complain, worry, and feel all the time that someone is doing something to us, or being mean to us, how will you or I know what is being said to us, if you or I spend every waking moment of our time complaining about life. I did not take on my son's challenge — it was not mine to deal with. It is my son's challenge to deal with. For a long time, fear took hold of my son's mind and heart. He never talked about how he felt when his dad left. All I know was he shut down when my ex-husband left. My ex-husband left when my son was three years old. First, he thought he was my husband, because daddy left. He used to let everyone who came across his path know that not only was he my husband, but also the girl's daddy. I thought at the time it was a joke, but as the years went on, he became troubled in his spirit and in his mind. I could see it in the kinds of friends he was attracting. They were much older than him, and he was not listening to me, but to his friends. Whatever his friend said to him was law in his mind and heart. I would plead with him about his friends that they were trouble because they are much too old for him to be hanging around with. I could see that shutting down would cost him a lot of pain in his life, but I could not help him. He had to help himself.

I have learned that I can support someone in what they are doing, and to let someone know that you are there mentally and spiritually. The emotions are that person's job to deal with. There is no one in this world that can meet your need but you. My son was looking for the other boys to fill his need. When my son and his friend got themselves arrested, he was seven years old. He became involved with the law.

That is when I knew something was wrong. At seven years old, he was in trouble with the law. I began to blame myself as a mother. I felt guilty because I had no husband, and I did not want to get a new husband just so that he could have a daddy. I started to give into his whims. The more I tried to protect him, the more he decided to give me a run for my money. I even sent him to a religious school thinking that would have prevented him from hanging out with his friends who I thought were no good company for him. I started to control his life to the point that when he cried, I was there wiping his nose and face. I did not want him to grow up.

My behavior told me today that I was playing the father of his soul. I became so protective and overbearing. I spoiled him thinking that I knew what was best for him. I held on so tightly, that I left him no room to breathe. What he was saying to me was to let go of him so that he can choose for himself what path he wanted to walk on — so he could learn the lesson for which his soul came to earth. I was afraid of letting him go, so I stood in his path, yet all the while I was so busy praying to God to help him. There was nothing I could do or say that would make a difference until he was ready to take responsibility for himself. The more I prayed, the more my son got himself in trouble with the law. He wanted to be my husband, and I went along with it, because at first it seemed like a joke, so whenever he said that he was the daddy around the house, I would laugh. I have since learned that it was not a laughing matter. The Spirit of the father was saying something to me through this three year old boy, but I was so caught up in my "poor me" syndrome that I was not hearing the boy crying out for help even at three years old. At the time when he was saying that daddy left and that he now is the daddy, I should have been more in tune with the Spirit of the father. "What is this saying all about? And how should I handle what is being said by this three year old?"

In 1972, I was struggling to keep a roof over our heads and clothes on our backs, and food on the table for five people. Yes, I was praying to God at the time for help, but it was not that kind of help I needed to pray for. I needed to ask the Spirit for guidance and direction on how to handle being a single mother without being so afraid of not being a good mom. Instead, I became so controlling to the children, that until this day, the hatred is still taking a long time to heal. The churches that I was involved in, were not teaching me how to approach God, because no one was really listening to God. It was all about what the pastor was saying in the Sunday service. I remember saying to a group of people that I do not think what my son was saying should be taken lightly, but in that prayer meeting, they thought that I was taking what my son said too seriously. He would outgrow what he was saying.

On growing up, my son was more challenging to me, by getting himself on the wrong side of the law. The more I prayed, the more my son and I were in court. I did not know at the time if I needed that kind of lesson. It was becoming apparent to me at the time, that if I was going to reside in Canada for a long period of time, and since I have the children, and being a black woman, I needed to know the spirit of the law.

The establishment of society sets the legal law from the old testament, which is the spirit of the law. There are also the words or the letters of the law. The lawmakers of today, are only using the letter of the law, and sometimes not even that. We cannot have one without the other. Therefore the Spirit which is Divinely directed is not being used in today's legal society.

Living in North America and the world is not just with the spirit of the law, but also the letter of the law. I was hiding my face behind the spirit of the law. What was happening to black people, especially mothers thinking like me — just praying alone is going to make everything right, and people will know that I am a religious woman. It helps, but without action, nothing will change, but I did not know that at the time. I wanted this boy at the time to obey and live the way I wanted him to live his life. The Spirit of the father was trying to get my attention and make me aware that there is another side to him and a life for me to live, and I was fighting the Spirit.

I was too afraid of Mary, even though I wanted to know the Spirit of the creator of heaven and earth since I was five years old. I only wanted to know what I did not know then — wanting to know is not good enough. Wanting to know must progress to knowing. At the same time, I ended up in the hospital fighting for my life with brain-hemorrhage, because the fear of the past of abuse and rape caught up with me. Also, at the time I should not have married my son's father, but I let my so-called room-mate tell me that God gave her a message for me to go back to my ex-husband. At the time, my room-mate was so convincing. I was alone and not knowing what to do, I gave in to the pressure of my room-mate and George, my ex-husband. I had just come to Canada three month's prior to my moving in with my room-mate. I had no one to talk to — I had left the nanny job, and I got a job working at Robert Simpson for the holiday. I left the church I was attending, and I could not tell anyone how I was feeling inside. I was afraid of everything that crossed my path to the point of no return. Life already took me down various paths, so that whoever came and said to me, God said, I would believe them.

My ex-husband and I were together and had three children in Jamaica in the West Indies. The three girls were back in Jamaica at the time. I had promised my mother that I would never take George back, no matter what happened to me in Canada. I was twenty-three years old in a place where I knew no one but Barbara, my room-mate. She was much older than I was, I thought that she really knew God, so I listened to her. I had allowed Barbara to dictate to me about God, which was never the truth. She knew that all I talked about was knowing God, and because she knew where my heart was, she used God to convince me to take back George. Looking back now, it was not Barbara's fault, it was mine. I was too bruised, hurt, and sad to listen to what the voices in my heart were saying to me. I allowed Barbara to find out my weakness about God, and she used that to get me back with George. I gave up my responsibility, and my accountability of my actions to have Barbara telling me what to do, and this was my life, not Barbara's. I have come a long way since then. I have learned some hard lessons because of my choices I had made back then.

The choice I made in 1968 produced a boy who was born in a sea of confusion, and George left me any way, and my son became father, or so he thought in is mind at the time, and I was too blind to see or listen to him, or the Spirit of the father .When George asked me to take him back, I should have been more forceful and had more courage to stand up to him and Barbara. I had told George, no, when he called me from Montreal in November of 1967. I told him people do not change over night. He kept calling and my answer was always no. It was not until January of 1968 when he came to Toronto and I met with him face to face, and he met Barbara, and even then I said no, because no one changes over night, and I knew that he was not changed. I went on to tell him that God had brought me from a place of hardship, walking with the Spirit of my redeemer. I did not know at the time why I gave in to him. I kept saying no until one morning George made breakfast and there was toast. I ate the toast and remembered saying, "Why is this toast tasting so funny," and he laughed. I later gave George his walking stick, and I was left to deal with my son and his challenge with the court and the three girls. I always believed that my son is here to remind me of consequences of not listening to the Spirit.

In 1967 when I came to Canada, I did not know at the time that I was on a journey or a path. I never understood that there was a purpose in this life for me and everyone on planet earth. There was nothing wrong with me wanting to know and walk with the Spirit. What I did not know was that there was a price to pay for that knowing. The school I call life had lessons for me to learn, and the lesson was to know something about how the Canadian law works. I never knew anything about the law in Jamaica, because I saw firsthand how the police operated, and so I had made up in my mind that I wanted nothing to do with police and the law. The universal Divine Law wanted me to learn about its law and principles of operation. If one is going to walk with the spirit, one has to be willing to learn all of life's lesson that have presented themselves. I needed to know the Canadian legal system which is called the law. I buried my face in religion, and hiding behind so-called religiosity — I was just fooling myself into thinking that I did not have a need to know about the legal system, here in Canada. Even if one does not have children, we should all know something about the legal system.

There are two laws in this world. One is the book of laws where a group of ill-informed people get together to protect what they think they own. This is what the Canadian legal system is all about. The book of the law is not for ordinary people like my son. It is for the few that have a great deal of material wealth to lose. That is why prisons and jails are built so that the ordinary human being works for nothing, so that the book of the law controls the world resources as their own.

The second law is, "The Divine universal Law" which controls even the book of laws. Not even the few who think they control all the world resources can disobey this law, because it eats at the very core of each man's being on planet earth. It is a spiritual connection to all of us — it makes us one. No one can get away from this law because it deals with the soul, and personality, which is on the inside or the "Conscience." No matter how much we think we are disconnected from the inside, something will always tug at our hearts, until we pay attention to what is going on on the inside. Even if he or she thinks they own the world, they can have it all, because that law goes wherever we go on such deep levels. One has to live with oneself, and sooner or later that law awakens the spirit in us to stand up inside and give an account for our actions which we created through our thoughts. I know that the religious people who call themselves Christians think this law is outside of themselves in the sky. I used to believe in that kind of thinking. In the meantime, my son was on his way to spend his life in jail or in the book of laws, because I thought, and believed that everything is outside of myself, and the only way to make changes is to pray to a Spirit outside of myself. I refused to be involved in the divine universal law, because it was scary to be outside of the book of law with the dos and don'ts, wrongs and rights, which not even the people who put this book together can keep.

It was then that I knew that I could not continue with, and in the book of the law. My son and all the others would be doomed to life's do's and don'ts, wrongs and rights, which the lawmakers themselves break to accommodate the few who think they are in control of the world's resources. Here is this Spirit wanting to teach me the lesson I needed to live, but I refused to come into alignment with that internal spirit. Through my son, I was forced to take my face out of religion, and stop hiding, and come in from the cold and learn what the word of the law is by being in that courtroom with my son. My son was too young to know what the spirit of the law was and still is, but it was for me to learn how man interprets the book of law for the few that have a lot of material wealth in their lives. Coming from Jamaica, I know how the doctors work the book of law for themselves. I know what the spirit of healing through man is all about, but I know nothing about the spirit of the word or the spirit of the true law, which is the divine intelligence of the mind and heart of the universe who created all living things on the earth. Another thing I learned in the Canadian school of life was about the spirit of divorce. When I got divorced in 1973, I was so afraid of the court, yet I knew that George was never a part of the plan for my life, but getting a divorce meant going to the court, and telling my part of this marriage to a courtroom full of people. That day, when I went to court, I stood up there to tell the truth, nothing but the truth so help me God. I felt like my world came to an end. The book of law gave me a piece of paper that said I was divorced from this man and I could marry another man in six months. All that did not make a difference to me, even when I got married again to some man who only married me to stay in Canada. It still did not touch me mentally until my son started to get in trouble with the law.

Nothing changes in one's life until one begins to deal with it on a mental, emotional, and spiritual level. Changes do not take place until the mind is challenged to make changes. All change must take place in the mind which is where all thought comes from. I since learned that the mind does all the planning — that was where the universal thought did all of the planning — through the thought process, no matter what is happening in one's life. Unless it is processed on a mental level, no change will take place. It took me a long time to learn that. In Jamaica, I knew about the spirit of teaching, and I love teaching, but I was not interested for the Spirit to teach me through my son what the letter of the word was and still is. I wanted to be left alone when the Spirit wanted to teach me about the letter of the law.

Dis-ease is a spirit of separation of the mind, soul and body. Just like how we separate the spirit of the law and the spirit of the word, so that the group who created the book of law can manipulate and control the masses that are too afraid to be accountable for themselves by thinking and taking action by asking the universe for help, rather than being manipulated into feeling lost and fearful of life. Then they could stay in their place and be the underdog. I am convinced that Man is arrogant enough to think that he or she can manipulate and control the universe, by creating dis-eases and deciding to look for cures through research, and to get the praise from other men. That is why we are still battling all kind of dis-eases like that of the heart, and the spirit.

The creator of the universe created man to ask questions, by talking to the Spirit which connects to the source, which is the Spirit. When I look at the trees, the sunset, the sea, the rivers, walking along the banks of the great rivers of the world, listening to great composers from the past and present, contemplating how the mountains stand for all eternity, when I see those great animals from the smallest to the greatest — in those moments, I feel like I am at home inside and I found the answer I have been looking for within myself. Man who was created by the same Spirit thinks that he now has a lots of money through the book of law by the collective who thought that being educated they would be able to make a lot of money. So if he or she becomes a doctor or lawyer, it would give them the power to manipulate and control by fear mongering. Then the masses of the people would trust the doctors or the lawyers to uphold the society by the letters of the law, through healing. Here we are putting our trust in man to heal all of our dis-eases through our body and mind with man-made medicine which we call pills.

Dis-ease is a disorder of the mind and spirit. Man has two parts to them — an inner-self that only the Spirit of the universe, the creator of the earth sees, called the soul. The outer part of us is what we see, where you and I can pretend to be a lawyer or a doctor, because we were trained to be a doctor by another man who trained us to think the way he was trained to think. This is how the book of the law trains us to think. The circle continues from one generation to the next. All this training that one goes through to become a lawyer or a doctor was set up in a way by society's standard of the book of laws. If I should go around and interview doctors and lawyers, they would tell you that their fathers or mothers wanted them to be lawyers or doctors so that they could make lots of money.

Medicine and law have nothing to do with healing, they are all about money. Healing is something else in the mind and heart of the people who are in those professions. The book of law was designed in a way for the masses to be dependent on the law and medicine — it is not for the purpose of truly healing man, because no man can heal our dis-eases without the full spirit of healing, which only the creator can do, by the spirit of love. The spirit of the law and the letter of the law are the same as being a doctor or a lawyer whose calling is to heal the soul and the heart through the creator's love. Without the love of the Spirit, no healing would take place in the soul. That is why dis-eases like Cancer, AIDS, heart, lupus, TB, Diabetes and all the others that man thought they had found cures for have returned. Those dis-eases were never cured — they were put on hold by taking a bunch of pills per-day to hold off the dis-ease, or just ease the pain. Being a doctor or a lawyer is about making money and living off sickness and dis-ease.

I do not believe that the creator wants us not to make a living. It is how we make that living and when we make the living through what we love, instead of doing it by the collective through the book of law, by the do's and don'ts. It is money, not really healing. As I said before, healing is by the spirit through the mind, and heart. There is nothing wrong with having money.

In this life and this society, we need the money to live. But living should not capitalize off sickness and dis-eases.

The word ease means freedom from pain, freedom from worry, trouble, anxiety, and stress. What does all this mean to the ordinary people who do not understand what all these eases mean to them — when they have to get up in the morning and start to think about providing for their families. It means that without the Spirit of the creator, there is no life. I knew that when I got the call about my son last summer about the possible threat of having Cancer, if it was 1970, I would not have been able to be calm and collective about the whole thing. I would be screaming and moaning to God, and asking why! I would be on the telephone crying to all my so-called friends — knowing full well that they could not help me nor fix or heal my son. When I got the news, I sat down at the table quietly for a while, without saying a word out loud to any one. I have learned to calm down and establish boundaries. The cancer scare was not happening to me. It was my son and I could not fix him — only the Spirit of the father could heal my son's lungs no matter what was wrong. I said, "Father, how do I handle this information about my son threat of lung cancer?" I do not even say God anymore when I am praying. I say, "Father, I know that only you can handle cancer, not me." I just prayed and asked the father to teach my son how to handle the information in his own way and to teach him how to handle his lungs in your way.

When I went to see the doctor in October, he said that my son did not have cancer, but his lungs were badly damaged. The doctor was puzzled about his lungs. My son had forgotten what had happened to him eight years ago. I believed that the father was saying something to my son. I believe that now he is thirty-one, he is old enough to talk to the father of love to help him with his lungs, knowing that a lot of people only use the outer man and do not look at what the inner man wants and needs. All these years I have been talking to the father for my son, and now it is his turn to talk to the Spirit for himself about his dis-ease, because he has been sleeping all these years. He has been sleeping since 1985 when I could not send him back to the boy school in the United States. From there, he picked up his old habit of punishing me — by hating me. Suddenly, I knew I had to surrender him to the father, and to let him speak to his heart, and to the depth of his soul or his own spirit. To me, having cancer of the lungs, or just having a hard time breathing is enough to hopefully wake him up from his fourteen years of sleep. I know no doctor can help him until he is awakened from his heart to know that he is not the only one in the world. Easing the pain is not enough. Denying and abandoning the pain will not work. Only by the Spirit of love will there be healing so that the symptoms will not be masked with pain killers. I know that cancer can be healed, but not by man, but by the Spirit of the lord. If we get down and dirty, and start to really do some purging from the soul and heart, mentally and emotionally, we will be made whole.

To be healed of all our dis-eases, one must first allow the Spirit of the father, or the creator to help him or her to dig out fear, hate, anger, sadness, and sorrow. I no longer feel the sadness I used to feel as I have learned to trust the Spirit of the creator who loves me unconditionally.

Today, we have a lot of names for a lot of things. People now are being called gay. I thought the word gay meant happy. Again, drunkenness now is alcoholism. Now there are pills for everything in this life that ails us. Most of us do not sit down and ask ourselves questions as to what we want out of life, and what is our purpose and calling in this life. There are so many things in this life that I am still learning, like being a better person, such as being kind, good, gentle to myself, so that I can be gentle to others in my life.

Something Is Wrong With Me

I used to think that something was wrong with me, because I allowed others to treat me like a doormat. I used to be such a nice person who wanted to please everyone. Since then, I stopped being a good person and became a nice person who wanted to please everyone. I became so nice that I stopped thinking for myself. When I came to Canada, I knew who Mary was, and one day I woke up and Mary was so nice that I stopped saying no. Instead, I said yes, even when I meant no. I got so nice that I really felt badly about myself, even though I wanted to know God. And I spent so much time searching for that inner person that I called God. I wanted to know the real God, the God that created heaven and earth, that lived on the inside of me, right in the seat of my soul and heart. The struggle that went on in my heart was killing me — my wanting to know the father of the creator who sent my soul to learn how to live and learn with other souls on earth, but I was not learning anything. All I ever heard was how stupid I was. The more I became nice, the more I felt stupid.

I have learned that there is a big difference between being nice and being good. This all started when I met Frank almost fourteen years ago. At the time, I was in need of money. I wanted to work but again, my son was sick, and I was not able to work outside the home. But I had a business designing clothes, making and selling them in a store on consignment. But enough money was not coming in to keep up with the rent. My lack of trust and lack of love always sat dormant until I was again in financial trouble. When I met Frank, I should have asked questions. I should have asked the Spirit if working for and with Frank was the best thing for me, and if Frank had my best interests at heart. I did not ask those questions, because I was always so desperate for money. I was on a panic roller coaster for money all the time. I did not ask if I had Frank's best interest at heart. I just jumped into his life and took over because I had to be in control. I did not ask the Spirit that I talked to all the time for help or to teach me how to treat Frank, rather than throwing myself in his life and then regretting it later. I was desperate for money, and all those old feelings that were never dealt with came back — the feelings of not being good enough, the feeling of something being wrong with me, came back. The sadness of my mother and father came back on top of my own challenges. Frank's needs were even greater. He had a lot of money but that was it. I wanted money and I felt at the time that God sent Frank to me for me to look after him and for him to pay me to do so. I was so thankful when I met him. He needed someone to do some sewing and mending work clothes. I took the sewing job, and the next thing I knew, I was working outright for Frank, sewing, cleaning, cooking, gardening, the whole works. Frank was a gardener, and he was almost sixty-five years old when I met him. He was never married — being single all of his adult life. Both himself and his mother shared a small bungalow. He needed some one to care for him; he was in bad shape, because for forty years he had not gone to see a doctor. Here was Mary who always wanted to fix others — instead of finding out why she always felt like something was wrong with her, and finding out where this feeling was coming from. I had just run from hospital to hospital with my son, and now Frank. Yes, I am in need of money, "But Father, Frank's needs are so great and I also have something wrong with me, because I am a nice person with something deadly wrong, I am always in need of money, and that's why I always have to move because of money problems. Father, with his need so great, I can do it?" I took Frank on thinking that my problems with feelings of not being worthy to be loved, would disappear. I had to take Frank with all his baggage — that full half-old envelope that needed to open, and looked inside. But Frank has never opened all his baggage, nor the envelope, much less look in those envelopes — I mean his life. All Frank knew was to work and save all his money.

I believe that Father gave me Frank with all that money to see what I would do with it. All my life I have had money, but I always gave it away to others. I did not know how I felt about giving Frank's money away. I just took Frank over like another child, and while Frank screamed, I just pulled away at Frank and his money, and it was not until it was all gone, or most of it, that I really understood I had a big problem on my hands. I was sobbing, knowing I was in big trouble with him. Frank was born with a mild touch of cerebral palsy. He could run his own company and was good at making money. I had a rude awakening coming to me. What I did not know at the time was that people do not have to use their hearts, just their head. I did not notice I was so resentful inside and full of sadness, and sorrow. I thought everyone was nice like me. I buried the pain of sadness and sorrow so deep, that I just felt that it was no use worrying about being good. I felt like I should just be nice to everyone and the world would be nice back to me. I am writing about healing my spirit and I wonder how I could have felt so badly about Mary, when I was in religion. I prayed and read my bible, so how is it that I did not look at me? I was too busy taking care of everyone instead of Mary. I was not loving Mary, I was too afraid of "the shadow" that was always hanging over me. I have learned since then, that all those feelings came from my childhood, and unless I look at those days and become aware of what can happen to people when something happens in their childhood, all those pains get pushed further and further in the subconscious.

Like the issue of money, I did not know why I always giving money away when I had it. All I knew was that I needed help with some deeper issues. Almost one million dollars was gone, and I did not buy anything for myself. Even the house that Frank and I owned together was gone. I needed answers and I needed it then. I went inside to find why all this money that God gave to me was gone so fast.

Childhood

I did not know that I was the manager of my life, and that mine was the only life I had to manage. I was so naive to think the people I met along the path of my life would manage my life for me. I did not want to lose the little girl inside, so I let someone else manage that little girl. There was abuse and that little girl never really took responsibility for her actions. Just because that child had to be an adult for her parents does not mean that she should not be responsible. I brought all those feelings of pain and abuse from my childhood into adulthood, and that was where dis-ease came from. The spirit of childhood pain, if not dealt with, can also cause dis-ease. Dis-ease as the word said, is the disconnection from the spirit. It is like the electricity — when it goes off we are all in darkness. That energy is what creativity is all about, and when that is disconnected, our lights go off. When we have unresolved issues that have never been looked at, no matter how we try, the pain will not go away. Sometimes a person who dies with unresolved issues I believe will come back to earth with all that pain that was never dealt with. I believe childhood cancer, and all those other diseases come from the past energy that the mother never dealt with. Maybe I am wrong, but with all the reading I have been doing, and with my own childhood's sixth sense, that is why I say that. I believe it was that feeling inside of me, why I thought something was wrong with me. Was something wrong with me? I do not think so now, but I used to feel so and think so. I gave everything away whether the person needed it or not, because I wanted to be loved and to belong. I never felt safe or belonging to anyone since I was a little girl. I felt life had treated me with a bad hand. Something must be wrong with me why I was always picking up men and women who are weak mentally and emotionally. Something must be wrong with me why I cannot stay in one place for long. I was always moving every year, when I had four children. Something is wrong with me when I do not know how to say no, but always yes when I should be saying no. I had such a deep sense of darkness and sorrow in my heart — the sadness was buried so deep into my subconscious. I did not know how to deal with this sadness, so I moved often, and blamed the landlord for treating me badly. Sometimes I could not pay the rent or when I could pay the rent, the house had to be cleaned and fixed up, and as soon as I fixed up the house, the landlord would put the house up for sale. When all this was happening to me, I thought I must have done something wrong. I still went to the religious institution for spiritual help, but I was still doing the same thing, and feeling the same way. I knew the feeling of sadness had controlled my life. I could not shake it off no matter how hard I prayed. I was convinced that something was wrong with me. I needed healing — I prayed all the time for healing and change would come for awhile and something would happen again, and that feeling of unworthiness, or the same old beating on Mary would come back. No one seemed to know how to help me to work out that feeling of something being wrong with me.

In 1985 I bought a house in Mississauga. At first it seemed like everything was going my way. I was thanking God for helping me to get the house. As soon as things were right enough to feel good about myself, I lost my job. Then the old Mary, and the feeling of something wrong with me returned. My something is wrong with me returned for me to deal with, which I did not know how to do. The fear of losing the house made me again feel that sense of loss, sadness, and sorrow. At night when I was alone in my room, I would talk to God about what was happening to me. I remember saying to God one of those nights, "Why am I going around in circles? What is wrong with me? Something must be wrong with me, because I cannot hold down a job long enough to get things done financially. I do not know what it is." I cried and prayed again and it seemed like there would be some change coming from where I do not know at the time, but whatever it was, I was still three long weeks at home without a job, and without the job there would be no mortgage. After three weeks of praying, I felt in my Spirit to go back to where I was working and ask back for the job without pay as long I got the paper to say I was working. I went and I got the job back.

I got the mortgage renewed on the house. I had been praying to God since I was a little girl for help. The children were now older, the middle and the youngest one were living with me at the time. The youngest girl and the older girl were in Ottawa at school. I spent so much energy on being afraid of losing a place to live because I did not want to have to deal with landlords. That's why I went and worked for two months free labor, so that I could get the mortgage on the house. I got the mortgage all right, but I had no job again. I thought they would at least let me stay on, but this woman had asked for the job for her niece. What am I going to do now I got the mortgage on the house? So I took some young people in from the Children's Aid to help me pay the mortgage until I got a job. But that was again the wrong choice — they were abused young people who were in need of love and care, and to top it all off, they were drug addicted. Some of them were young men who had been to jail for drugs. I did not know how to help them, but I just prayed for them not to sell the drugs in the house. The fear of losing the house to these drug addicted young people just made it worse, because at the time what I did not know was that nothing was wrong with me. I just did not realize that my childhood pain from my mother and father were what I needed to look at from the inside of my heart. Even though I was praying to God for help, I really did not know how to help Mary from being sad and feeling sorry for herself. I had learned since I was seven years old from my broken spirited mother, who was lost without my Papa. To get help, one needed to be a victim. Playing the victim was the game I saw my mother play to get Papa's attention. I was seven years old when I went to school and, prior to that, I went to the primary school. Shortly after I started school, the 1951 hurricane came and we lost everything we owned. My mother was so devastated over the loss of her material things, and to make things worse, my papa left us to put back the pieces together. My mother could not do that — she needed my Papa to do it for her. Papa was not around, so I started to work and put the pieces of my mother's life together. I was able to go to school while I worked to support my family.

My mother became my child and responsibility. At the time, it was five of us brothers and sisters. One day, when the school reopened, we were all in class when my schoolmates told me that my mother was crazy, and the people in the village were planning to put her away, and that my sisters and brothers and I would go to an orphanage. I would not be able to be so good in school, and I would not be able to show off how bright I was, because I would have to work all the time, and I would not go to school. I just made a loud scream in school, and ran out of school to go to my mother's. She was sitting at the roadside looking so lost like a little girl, that I felt sorry for her. I looked at this lost woman who was my mother, and who was so helpless, that I just took her by her hand and lead her home to clean her up. My mother had the most beautiful head of hair. I did not notice that my mother did not comb her hair for weeks. That was hard for a seven-year-old girl to make sure her mother was taken care of. I combed her hair, I gave her a bath, and I made her a cup of tea. And I looked her in the eyes and said, "Mama, I will take care of you, but you will have to help me." I told her that the villagers were planning to put her away, so she needed to help me. I knew that I would have to work hard. The sadness and sorrow came from that day when I was seven and saw the sadness in my mother's eye. I felt sorrow for her. I was working with my mother for a whole year and working to put our lives back and to repair the damage that was done by the hurricane to the house when Papa returned and my mother sent me packing. I know where the sadness and the feeling of sorrow came from. Papa came back to my mother and she took him back and put me out. It was betrayal and rejection by both of them that I took on myself for all those years that were buried so deep in the soul which gave me the feeling of liking to be needed all the time.

CARE Giver — That is the part of the my personality I really show to the public, because that was the way life was for me when I was a little girl, being my mother's mother. I made sure my mother was being cared for until the day she died. I was twenty-four years old, and living in Canada when she died. When I reached deep into my soul and found out that nothing was wrong with me, I felt that sense of sadness lift from my soul. Once I took a look at why I always wanted to be needed and why I was attracting immature men who were too afraid of their own shadow, and only looking outside of themselves, I knew that I was learning to look inside and they only wanted to look outside like my ex-husband. I started to work on myself fourteen years ago.

I started to work on myself in 1980 when I went to live in Richmond Hill, Ontario, where I met a schoolteacher whose name was Olga. She was a single mother who was involved with TM - Transcendental Meditation. That was my first encounter with religious changes. Olga told me that I was in need of healing to my spirit, and no one could do it for me but me. At first I was afraid to meditate with her because it was new to me. I knew how to talk to God. I learned about talking to God or praying from an early age.

Meditation was something talked about in religious circles. I used to sit and pray, and sometimes I would not say anything but stay quiet. I did not know that was what meditation was all about until I met Olga. I did not go to the group with her because my son was in school in the United State, and at the time I was in need of all the money I could get to keep him in school. What Olga and her son would do was to teach me how to meditate. She told me that if I was afraid of the changes, I should pray until I got used to the new way. She told me to have a mantra to say over and over again in the form of prayer. What I did not know then, that prayer and meditation must be processed mentally, emotionally and spiritually. Olga told me that I had so much negativity in my life, like fear of sadness in my heart? She said that was why I had the brain hemorrhage. She told me it was time to start working on myself so I could feel whole. She did not care how I did it, as long as meditation became all of my life. Olga told me to find a scripture to meditate on every day. I knew that all of my life up until then, I wanted to know God and serve him, but I was not taught how to do that unless I went to bible college which I had attempted to do in the sixties, but could not abide by the rules. Man, and not the Spirit made up the rules. Going to bible college would never let me know God. I found out for myself, by meditation that going to bible college is another way of conforming to religion, and that was not the way to know God. Knowing God must come from my heart and not from my head. I have learned how to open my heart and soul to the Spirit of the creator, by meditation. If I can do that every day, I will know God, and serve him in a way that man cannot show me to do. After being with Olga and meditating with her every night, something in me was changing and Olga got afraid of me. She did not want me to pray around her any more. Her son used to come and talk to me and she stopped him from coming. The feeling of rejection was there, but not like before. When someone says or does something to me, that sadness and sorrow would come back, but not in such a powerful way like before. Now I not only pray, but I also meditate. Real healing was taking place in my heart and soul. Olga did not believe in praying, just meditation. I have learned since then that I cannot have one without the other.

Medication versus Meditation

Medication — does it have anything to do with healing? I do not think so, yet it is our motto today. Medicate yourselves so as not to feel what is inside of our souls. We no longer as people trust the Spirit of the creator, or trust ourselves for healing. We left it all up to the doctors who are human beings like us. Yet they are the modern God, and the savior of the world to heal all of our dis-eases. They have all the answers for what ails and pains us. Modern man has become a junkie for legal drugs to medicate the fear of the unknown.

There are drugs or (pills) for everything that the modern man feels. For instance, the drug industries have something for brains or the mind; heart, liver, lungs and the list goes on and on, but nothing for the spirit. It is the spirit that is in need of healing first, not the body, yet we spend billions of dollars feeding and medicating our bodies just not to feel the anger and fear of the past in our soul. Man has not learned anything of the past history of what can happen to a people that forget that there is spirit within man that no medication or drug will ever quench the thirst for truth, trust, peace, joy, meekness, kindness and gentleness. That is what the Spirit requires.

Why do we replace our spirit for doctors to take care of our bodies? Being a doctor was never meant to replace the Spirit of the creator which I call father. Why have the doctors become God? Doctors were taught by others how to look and care for dis-eases in the body, but doctors should never replace God. Doctors, like drugs have become commodities like the carmakers and food producers. Society built in its establishment a collective of people who form and program our mind from a young age to believe in only what we see. What we see has nothing do with how we feel.

I believe there is a spirit that roams the world and convinces man into thinking that they can change the universe, by calling themselves scientists. They are the God of the world and that is how very slowly they were able to convince people to trust them, because they can never see the spirit. Man has been taught to become doctors where they can dispense tremendous power over others who are valuable. For the last fifty years we have built the establishment that has built hospitals (drugs factories) to hold people who are supposedly sick in bodies and in minds. By housing these people, the dis-eases of all kinds had risen in a way that the system that was built to help the sick was now falling apart, because it was built on the illusion of foolish men who had big ideas.

In 1981, I went to Los Angeles for my holiday to visit my friend and his family. I got a job as a movie critic, and I could not take it because I had a job to come back to. Working with my friend, I felt that I should resign from my job in Canada and take the offer that presented itself to me. I did not take it, I came back to Toronto. For weeks I contemplated leaving the job and finally gave in and stayed. I felt in my spirit that something was wrong, but fear took over, because I had to pay my son's tuition. He was in the United States in a boarding school. One month later, I was out on my back, and out of a job and no compensation because none of the women that worked with me would witness the injury.

For weeks I was in bed, and one morning, I got up to answer the door. There was my neighbour Olga, who was away and did not know what was going on and who had not seen me for awhile and came to check. For a whole year she has been trying to teach me how to meditate through TM, and I refused because I was too afraid of what I did not understand. My neck and back were hurting, and right then and there she said, "You are going to pray and meditate." I knew the bible talked of meditation, but I really thought it was repeating the prayer over and over. Olga said that the reason why so many people are so sick was because they are too caught up with doctors and medication. She told me to stop talking and sit quietly and take deep breaths, and in doing so, the body would relax and I could find my way to my soul, or the spirit. I was praying but it was not enough, and even though I wanted to know God, I did not know how to bring my mind and soul together to make me a whole person. I used to talk about my doctor like he was a God, and he could save me from all that ailed me. It is status quo to hear people talk about their doctors like they were the creator of the universe. Sometimes, I had to ask the question, "What about you? What do you think? And why am I not thinking for myself?" I realized that without meditation and prayer there is no healing. I also realized that I stopped meditating on the things of God and Olga had to remind me of what I used to do. We ask the doctor who is man himself, who only knows how to help us cover the pain with medication, so that we would not have to feel what is going on on the inside. Meditation helps us get to the root of what ails us from the inside, because it is the spirit that is in need of healing. With all the challenges I have faced, and all the prayers I have said over the years, I have learned that I did not have a relationship problem, or money problem, or even dis-ease. What I did have was a spiritual problem. The problem with the houses, the problem with money, it was only a way to get my attention to stay on the path of learning. I now believe that everyone on earth has come to learn something, and to do so we must first find out what it is we need to learn. I did not know all that, until I met Olga. I had a lot of teachers over the years since I was two years old, but lack of understanding did not permit me comprehension of what was being taught to me. I have learned that life is a process, and it takes time to process life's lessons. The soul needs to learn and grow, and we humans have to give the spirit time to process its journey. A long time ago, I thought I was in love with my doctor, and whatever he said and did was the gospel. It was not until I was in the hospital lying on my back where I was alone, with no one coming to see me, that I had no choice but to start to listen. I gave myself permission to talk to God. I was reading the bible but I was not practising what it was saying to me. I could not do what the bible said. My heart was filled with pain from the past, and no doctor could heal a heart that is filled with fear and sadness. I was reading all kinds of religious books, but I was not doing what needed to be done to bring changes to my life.

Meditation and prayer combined are what will bring changes from the inside. I have learned since then, that true healing only takes place when the heart is filled with love from the creator of the universe. Healing must come from the heart, soul and mind. The doctors cannot do it for you or me; we have to hear the Spirit, by listening to the body and the heart. I was so afraid of listening to my heart. I did not want to hear what was being said. I did not know that something was going wrong in my head. I refused to stop and take time out for me to listen to my body. There was so much chattering going on in my head, that I could not hear what the Spirit was saying in my heart. I had to stop being so afraid of my ex-husband. I felt like the whole world was against me, and the next thing I knew, the brain was bleeding and almost killed me. It was not my brain that was in trouble, but my whole being. If I did not listen I probably would have never walked again. Lying in the hospital, I got time on my hand to listen and hear what the Spirit of the creator was saying. That is the Spirit within all men, and wherever men go, the Spirit is there. The spirit will not do anything without you or me. People can pray to God for help for them to do this or that, but what we do not know is that God will not do for us what we can do for ourselves. The father will open the doors and we have to walk through it. Men have been taught that the Spirit or father or God is in the sky somewhere. That is not true, it is false doctrine. The Spirit is on the inside of man, and that is how the Spirit of the creator planned life to be. That is why man thinks that the body is separate from the spirit.

Once I found out that I needed to start over again talking or praying the way I used to pray when I was a little girl, I made a vow to the Spirit of the father, that I will always talk to it first, before I talked to anyone. Most of us are afraid to listen to ourselves, or make our own decision when we do. We will have no one to blame but ourselves. We humans like to blame someone else for what has gone wrong in our lives. Every time I am in trouble with my health, I know that the father is trying to get my attention. Being in the hospital reminded me of when I was twenty-one years old, living like the rest of the other people. I loved to sit on the fence, so that no one could hold me responsible for making unwise choices.

When I was fourteen years old, I lived beside a big church, and when my aunt was not watching, I would go and sit on the fence to hear what the preacher was saying. By my sitting on the fence, I only heard half of what was being said about God. I was afraid of my friend who thought I was too young to want to know God at the time, so I stayed on the fence. In that way no one could accuse me of not being a religious person. The one thing I needed to learn was to know how to love with all of my heart, mind and soul. Once I learned to love, there was nothing in this life to be afraid of but fear itself. I was afraid of everything pertaining to life. What I was afraid of was Mary, because I did not know what my life's purpose was, or what the spirit of the father wanted of me. I did not know my purpose or my calling in life. I was not listening. I found out that I did not trust me, nor love me. So how could I hear from God? Another thing I learned, in order to love someone, my heart must not be contaminated with fear, anger, sadness, sorrow and hate. The reason why we do not hear from God or listen to the Spirit is because our hearts are filled with everything except love. Contaminated hearts cannot trust or tell the truth. It is the same thing like peace. If peace is not with our awareness, like prayer with meditation, our lives are contaminated and there can never be forgiveness.

Dis-eases and sickness will always be here unless we make changes and begin to live the life the Spirit of the father wants us to live. By processing life through love, peace, truth and trust, God wants wise people. Wise people are people that can think for themselves, and who are willing to take responsibility for their actions — and they believe that wisdom is from the Spirit of the creator. They realize that taking care of themselves helps so they can listen from their hearts to hear what the body is saying. I have learned that wise people do not blame others for what has happened to them, but will take the time out to sit quietly, and meditate and ask questions. What lessons do I need to learn from what is happening? I know I cannot fix whatever is happening in my life at the time. I know the Spirit of the creator can make all things right. No man can. So, when I talk about medication verses meditation, that is what I really mean. One is from man, and the other from the Spirit.

Most of the time what is really causing pain or what we think is causing pain is not real. When you or I go to the doctor and he or she gives us medication for the pain or for the cancer, or for whatever it is, it is only a cover for what is really going on inside of the heart. I have learned that the doctor is trained by man, so he or she does not know about how you feel unless you or I tell them. Only you or I know how our bodies work, and only the Spirit can heal when our hearts are in the place of love. We are spirit, living in a body on earth. God gave us this body when we came to earth to fulfill its work. We have more than a body, mind and personality. Most of all, we have a spirit which we call soul.

Our responsibility is to take time to get to know how the body works. We need to think and feel good inside so that we can keep the body dis-ease-free. We need the Spirit to help us learn about our bodies. Listening is so important, but we mostly like to talk, just like me. I have learned the art of listening. I would ask myself, "Why don't I listen to my heart, what am I afraid of?" I found out that I was afraid to be alone with myself. Most of us are not prepared to learn about ourselves, because we are too afraid of making change. Most of us hate change, so we go around in circles all the time by hiding in religion, or behind our work, families, children, husbands and wives. We go from one sex partner to another or from one relationship to the next, which we know is not good for us. But we do it anyway.

I married a man that personally was not good for me. He had so much baggage that he carried over from childhood coupled with mine that we buried deep in our hearts. It could fill Air Canada Center. I married this man thinking that I could fix him or change him into what I wanted him to be. Like I was God! I was playing God, wanting to fix him. After he was gone, I started to hide behind the children until I found myself on my back. I almost let life take care of my body instead of me, because I felt helpless, with my "poor me" attitude. Or I made people think that I was helpless so that I did not have to do it for myself. I knew religion could not heal my soul or my spirit — no man on Planet earth has that kind of power to do so. Yes! There is no medication in this world that is ever going to heal the spirit, no matter how hard you or I try, or what the doctors do. Only the Spirit of the father can fix our lives, and only when we ask for help. We will never get rid of dis-eases out of this world, or out of our lives in our lifetime. We are too dependent on man to heal us and all our dis-eases. We have medication to fix all that ails us, but there is nothing in this world that can heal the spirit, but the Spirit.

Alternative Medicine

Alternative medicine is made from herbs. The conventional drug is made from synthetic drugs. Most of their base is from real Herbs, but today most of the drugs on the market are made from synthetic material. They have real bad side effects on the body. Even with alternative medicine, the dis-ease of cancer and all the other major dis-ease will not go away. There seems to be no cure, because human beings are not ready to trust the Spirit of the soul and heart for real healing. Many people are turning to Herbal medicine for their health, but there will not be any help unless you and I are connected to the source. The Spirit of the creator is all we have to help us and all we have to trust about how we feel inside, and to know that healing comes from the inside of our being.

Trust

I have learned something about trust. I have never trusted anyone, because I have never trusted myself. I did not know how to think or feel. Most of us do not really trust anyone, because we do not trust ourselves. Trust is a big thing for most people in our world today. What I have learned is that I do not have trust problems with other people. I have trust problems with myself. The word trust means to make a choice and think for oneself, and I must listen to the spirit to make those internal and external decisions for myself. I also learned that there is a difference between putting my trust in God and in myself, than putting my trust in someone else. I now trust the Divine that people will do the right thing in their hearts, by honoring what they said they would do. The word trust means action — when someone puts what they said into action, that is trust. It is mentally, emotionally and spiritually to be processed from the heart. It is not an intellectual word alone, it is a spiritual word from the heart and soul. Trust is life — life is a journey, but lately I have learned it is not a journey alone, but also a process in our being. It comes with a road map, and a compass. I have learned that the road map is the heart, and the compass is the mind, and we need the map and the compass to work together so that we can trust that the path you and I are traveling on is a spiritual one. And no one can tell us where to go and what to do on this journey, but the Spirit. I had read the book *Mr. God this is Anna*. The little girl said, "Mr. God works from the inside, and if we trust from the inside then there is no fear." Fear is why we do not trust, and trust is not knowledge. It is the ability to step out of the way from the inside with love. Love comes from trust and truth. Truth gives way to the spirit of trust.

In 1972, I went to New York City to sing in this church, and I had to get up early Monday morning to catch a plane back to Toronto so that the children could get to school for nine o'clock. We were rushing to catch the plane and the children had breakfast, which they never ate so early in the morning. My youngest daughter got sick on the plane. I was so frightened that I made a promise to God at the time, that I would never go and sing until the children grew up. After I finished reading the book, I cried. I had never had a soul cry in a long time until that Saturday when I sat and read that book. I realized that I gave up the spirit of trust so that I could not fulfill my calling. I love to talk. I have been talking since I can walk, and now I have put it on hold for the time being. Trust is being in the moment and that has to come from the inside. I thought that trusting people is being spiritual, but it is not true, not unless you can trust yourself first. One thing I have learned in the last six years is that change must be mentally and emotionally processed before we can come to terms with whatever it is that we have to change in our lives. When you or I are lacking in truth, trust and love, there cannot be any peace in our souls. Because of the lack of love, truth and trust can make us think something is wrong with us. I thought something was wrong with me, I wanted to be healed — there was so much lacking in my life. I had to find out what was wrong with me from the inside.

Reconciliation or Reconcile

The meaning of reconciliation is to forgive, to settle a disagreement, or a quarrel, to make consent or to make content or acquiesce. Forgiveness is part of reconciliation, or inclination to forgive, pardon, to give up resentment against or the desire to punish, to pardon, to cancel, to reconcile to God or the creator of the universe, meant to become a friend again with love.

My father lived until he was eighty-six. He had never really been sick, because he never really held anything or anyone in his heart. I want to do the same. My father had a secret, he never held malice. He just said his piece to whoever had done him wrong. My father was a free spirited man who loved life. He always had a smile for everyone that he met along the way. He loved nature and he never went to church. He used to say, "God is the energy that makes everything grow and stay well."

Reconciliation requires a great deal of forgiveness on a level where only the Spirit could do that. So, when the people in South Africa are talking about reconciliation, they are talking about a healing that only the creator can do. Not Mandela, or Desmond

Tutu, but the Spirit of the creator. All black people want is equality and to be treated with total respect where no one sees colour, but people. I do not think that we black people can forgive the white people of this world to that extent. If we do, we would not be alive. I lent a few people Frank's money and they never repaid it. One of them was my good friend. Since I was sixteen years old, I had to ask the Spirit to help me realize that it was only money, it was not my soul. I have learned since then what it takes to forgive someone. Forgiving my friend does not mean that it was okay not to pay the money back. What it said to me is to let it go, release her so that my spirit could grow to full potential, so that reconciliation could take over. By my doing that, I could talk to her with love from my heart like I used to do before the money challenge came up. I am struggling to live, and so is my friend, but what about the children that are dying with AIDS and whose parents are already dead from the dis-ease. There can be no real reconciliation until White people of this world change – those who hold the wealth in their hands, and keep it for themselves, especially in South Africa where diamonds and gold built Europe and the western world.

Millions of people who they think should not be getting the proceeds from selling the Gold and diamond. No matter what man does, dis-ease and sickness will not disappear from us. Same thing with reconciliation, because only the Spirit of the creator can forgive the people of the White establishment of South Africa. Only the Spirit can create newness of mind, heart, and soul.

"Father," you are the law maker, and only you can make real reconciliation work in South Africa. Help us, your people to know that, and that all men are created equal in life. Heal us and the Land, and remind us every day that we do not own the land."

"The Land is the Lord's and the fullness thereof." (The Bible)

Chapter 7

The Economy

What does the economy and economics have to do with healing the spirit? It has much to do with people. Since the industrial revolution, people have been told that if they work hard and play hard, everyone will get rich. Without even taking time out to think of what the cost would be, the people went along blindly with the establishment of the day. After WWI, there was a lot of money made, and people invested in the stock market. Then came the crash in 1929, and many people lost their livelihood on the market, and killed themselves. And lots rebuilt again. Then came WWII, and people's lives were crushed again. No matter what position you were in life at that time, the war touched you. Yet, with all that happened since the industrial revolution, the economy was what drove people to trust the governmental establishment. The people, including myself in some way, put our trust in establishments to provide jobs, housing, food and medical care in some way for us.

Peoples' lives intertwine with the economy, mentally, emotionally and spiritually because of the way economics was set up. Yes, the economy affects our lives in a way that work and money is all that people live their lives for.

Everywhere I turn, I see construction of buildings going on, yet, when I listen and watch the news, all I hear is how bad the economy is. Is life that bad? Or, are the people being manipulated to believe that things are bad — that the world is in recession? Fear has become a plague to people's psyche — like Cancer. What does the economy have to do with fear and healing? Economics has a lot to do with people's lives in today's market as it is based on how and what people do in their lives. There are buildings of all kinds in our neighbourhood. I had to stop and ask the question, "What's wrong with this picture of the world about the economy? Why is there so much propaganda about the economy and the stock market? Why is the so-called government sitting back and letting the propaganda continue?" I believe the world leaders want the economy of the world to fall, just so that they can take full power and total control of the people.

The leaders of the world have sat back for a long time and made the underground or the sub-government, who make all the decisions of the world to breathe fear into people. They know that most people work from their heads, or from the personalities. The others work from their emotions and only few of us are conscious of what is going on around us. The powers of the world want it so. Fearing the economy is like having cancer or any other dis-ease where people's hearts fail them. That is what the end of the world will be like.

We are in need of healing... If we do not get healing for the economy, fear, anger, and control will be the winner. I believe all the conscious-minded people should get together and call on the Spirit of the Creator, whom I call Father.

Society has build great universities for learning, but the higher learning does not come from the heart. Some are trained to use only their minds. Others are trained to use only their hearts. We are so fragmented, it is scary. We have become robots without knowing it. For the last fifty years, the Government has been pushing education.

Every one needs to know how to read, and that is great, but what is the use of knowing how to read and write when it is not our free will. It is the will of the government. The people embrace everything that the government has said — like gospel. They will provide all kinds of services for the people. And now the talk is that the economy is in trouble. That is why there are so many people homeless, and so many others looking for jobs, because of the downsizing that took place in the early 1990's that left people more afraid of the future.

I believe that there is a power greater than man, and that only that power can fix the world economy — so that economics will not be played around with as currently is occurring. Economics is a game, and a gamble, and it is not life. Real life is not a game, because it is from the spirit and the soul. I know that if one continues to put trust in the external forces of this world, one's life will diminish right before one's very eyes, and there is nothing we can do about it — absolutely nothing.

The earth is the Lord's and the fullness thereof. And all that dwell therein. If all of us become spirit-born and see everything on earth, why would the Spirit allow man to destroy the earth.

We must remember the sun still sets in the west and rises in the east. No one has ever seen the wind when it blows. Man only feels it. Man might know the direction it's blowing but he will never, never see the wind. Another thing we the people of the world must remember is that, there are four seasons and they are co-ordinated — even though man would like to change the seasons to please himself.

Chapter 8

Psalm 91

He that dwelleth in the secret place of the most high shall abide under the Shadow of the Almighty. I have been reading this psalm since God knows when. Yet, I have never thought of this psalm in the way I do now. The Shadow" came to me to tell me to entitle my book, *The Shadow* in 1982 when fear, anger, and sadness were my life. I had lost my job through an accident at work and I never received any compensation. I was so angry at the spineless women supervisors I was working with at the time. They were afraid of losing their job. They never signed the paper that said I got hurt on the job.

When I was told in the winter of 2000 to write the book on healing it was to be based on the "Shadow of the Almighty." The psalm says, in my interpretation, that anyone who puts their trust in the Spirit of the father, Creator of the universe, or God as we call it, and whoever pursues truth about the Spirit of the father, will always be safe in a space where no one can touch them, because the creator of the universe will put a hedge around them as he did for Job. They will always be protected and feel a sense of safety.

Verse 2:

I know I will be protected from the storms of life no matter what is going on around me. The Spirit of the father will be there, because he knows I am depending on him for my shelter in a secure place in my heart, soul, and mind. My mental and emotional place will be so.

Verse 3

The Spirit of the father, the Creator of the Universe will always protect me from all mean spirits of my fellow human beings who are afraid of life and themselves who are filled with anger, envy, and jealously of all kinds. But, as long as I honor the Spirit of the father with love and not with the spirit of fear, anger and shame, my peace of mind will not be destroyed.

Verse 4:

As long as I honor the Spirit of the father with truth, trust, prayer, meditation, willingness, creativity, peacefulness and simplicity, nothing will ever affect my health or whatever I am doing, because the Spirit of the father and the spirit of truth become as one when my body will be protected from cancer, AIDS and from all diseases.

Verse 5:

Nothing that comes up against my shelter, or my hedges, or my covering, or where I live in my community will affect me. My house will be safe because the Spirit of the father will abide in and around my house. I will not be afraid of the neighbours whether by day or night. I will be safe and secure in that sacred place in my soul.

Verse 6:

When destruction or disaster come upon the land, nothing will touch the people who put their trust in the Spirit of the father. I am honoring the lord, the Spirit of the father with trust, and he will protect me mentally and emotionally.

Verses 7&8

Even though a thousand so-called friends come pretending that they are my friends, the Spirit of the father will never let them destroy me. They will fail because the creator of the universe is watching over, and keeping his eyes on me. No one will be able to take away my joy and peace, because the communion with my creator is my strength.

Verses 9&10

The Spirit of the creator and of the father will always shelter me, as long as my heart and my soul are connected to the source of its love. I was created in the love of the creator, and with love to love. I should not put my trust in man but in the Spirit of father.

Verses 11&12:

The Spirit of the father will put the angels in charge of the people who are in tune with the Divine law. That law allows the angels to become the watchmen over the mental, emotional, and the spiritual consciousness of the soul. When the day to day challenges present themselves to those children, the Divine guides them into its path by carrying them, so their feet or souls will not touch the ground.

Verses 13&14

The Spirit of the father will give you or me the strength and courage to overcome even the lions and dragons that are so strong and dangerous to our mental life. Yet, I know that we cannot do it on our own, without the Spirit sending the angels to prevent the powers of the world from controlling and crushing our movements in life. The Spirit of the father, the creator of the universe will fill our hearts with his love, to live as human beings who are walking on the spiritual path to a higher level of consciousness because it knows our name. The higher level of consciousness occurs when the mind stops being religious and becomes spiritual, so that my soul can learn through the Divine love. When the Spirit speaks, I can hear what he is saying to me. I can respond through prayer and meditation. The Spirit will always be with me when I am faced with a challenge, and will deliver me through Divine love. The Spirit will teach me how to honor the Divine law within my soul as long as I fulfill all the requirements by walking on the spiritual pathway.

As I think about healing and the spirit of healing, I realize that the reason why no diseases will enter my body is because my spirit is connected to the source of the Spirit of the father. The angels of the father will then stay close at all times around the children of the father as the creator is obligated to protect the creature.

As I continue to honor the Father in prayer and meditation, he will carry me on his shoulder and by his hand. My soul will always belong to him. Even though strong physical lions will come to destroy me, I will be able to stomp on them with the strength of the father. Even the young lion and dragon that are so mighty and who try to kill my spirit, for example, like the police and the lawyers who thought that they were taking my soul away from me, could not because it was only things they took, not my spirit. They could not destroy me because I am trusting in the Spirit of the father with his love. Because his love is all around, I have learned to honor myself. When I learn to honor myself as much as I honor the Spirit of the father, everything will be alright. I will be able to stand upon the light in my soul.

Wherever the Spirit of the father sends me, I go. I am here to love and serve the lord with all my heart and soul. I found out my purpose on earth is to pursue the vision of my soul. The Spirit of the father will guide and direct me, and most of all protect me in whatever I do, and enable me to serve my brothers in love. Nothing can break my spirit of love, truth, and trust for the Spirit of the father, the creator of the universe. With love, truth, joy, trust and peace, I will honor the Spirit of the father.